Countryman Press   2/10/09
                        34.99

                1991

                10~1   Photo 7.

(225)   03051905

North Country Gourmet

A Vermont Chef Cooks at Home

North Country Gourmet

A Vermont Chef Cooks at Home

ROBERT J. TITTERTON

The Countryman Press
Woodstock, Vermont

The Countryman Press, Inc.
P.O. Box 175
Woodstock, Vermont 05091

Library of Congress Cataloging-in-Publication Data

Titterton, Robert J.
    North country gourmet : a Vermont chef cooks at home / Robert J. Titterton.
      p. cm.
    Includes bibliographical references and index.
    ISBN 0-88150-203-0 (cloth)
    1. Cookery—Vermont.   I. Title
    TX715.T613 1991
    641.59743—dc20   91-24959
                                                          CIP

Printed in the United States of America

10 9 8 7 6 5 4 3 2 1

Cover and text design by Virginia L. Scott

Cover photograph by Didier Delmas

For Susan

Contents

✦

Preface

✦

Twenty years ago I came to Vermont to study at the State College in Johnson. Perched atop a hill, the campus commanded a panoramic view of the Lamoille Valley: green pastures, dark pines and maples crowded on hillsides, and a black ribbon of a river traced along the valley floor. It was the most beautiful place I had ever seen. I thought so even when arctic storms blew out of Canada and during mud season when the bottoms fell out of the roads. Vermont makes you think about where you live every day. After college, I left to attend culinary school in Rhode Island, married a wonderful woman, and have lived ever since in Elmore, Vermont, working for over a decade as saucier, and then chef, in two of the leading kitchens in one of Vermont's premier resort towns.

My longtime interest in history encouraged me to search out the roots of Vermont cooking. Initially I found books such as Lucy Emerson's 1808 *New England Cookery* that yielded simple Yankee foodstuffs prepared to keep half the year without refrigeration. Recipes were tersely worded, instructing the cook to "prepare in the usual way" and then to "bake until done." I soon discovered that the same recipes appeared, almost unchanged and without further elaboration, in books for nearly two hundred years. I wondered what had happened to the influence of the French who settled among the Abenaki Indians before English immigrants arrived. And what of the nineteenth-century waves of Northern Italians and French Canadians who came to work the quarries, railroads, and mills while the Yankees left in droves for Western frontiers? You'll find traces of their influence in some of my recipes—the French and French Canadians in such recipes as Venison Pâté and the Northern Italians in Escallops of Veal with Chanterelles, among others.

In addition to exploring the contributions of these groups to what has come to be known as Yankee cooking, I searched out foods that are grown locally or can be found in the wild—here and in most of the colder regions of North America—and emphasized these indigenous ingredients in my recipes. The result, I believe, is a contemporary cuisine with its roots in this region still so affected by its mountainous terrain, long, severe winters, and brief growing season.

Living as I do in a rural area and working in the resort town of Stowe is a good combination. There is time for the garden, foraging for chanterelles, fiddleheads, and tiny crimson strawberries, fishing for brook trout, or cross-country skiing on snow-covered fields in winter. At home my cooking experiments are more relaxed, away from the confusion and pressures of a professional kitchen.

At a restaurant the chef is responsible for countless details besides cooking. To manage all the tasks requires study and practice as well as experience and skill. Chefs do not have secrets or tricks. Everything is learned the hard way, usually after many attempts, cuts, and burned fingers. It is a difficult process since true professionals do not follow recipes; food is prepared by touch, taste, color, timing, smell, and intuition. The most satisfying outgrowth of working as a chef is sharing the experience with others. This is what I hope to do in this book by presenting my favorites among the recipes I have developed—the ones I most like to cook at home—and by explaining on the basis of my experience why things work and why some don't.

I hope you will enjoy these recipes which have grown out of my experience in Vermont. Most are my own creations. Those with familiar names have been improved by changing ratios and methods or by enhancing them with additional ingredients. All are dishes that, while shaped by insights gained from years in professional kitchens, can be readily prepared at home. Some recipes are simple, and others are more complicated, but all are explained in clear language. To encourage novice cooks to attempt any recipe, I have tried to anticipate questions that arise during preparation. At the same time, I address questions raised by experienced cooks on a wide range of subjects. I hope that everyone will find this contemporary North Country cooking appealing and altogether delicious.

Elmore Mountain
February, 1991

North Country Ingredients

✦

Vermont's traditional cookery, like that of most of North America's colder regions, was born of necessity. A frost-shortened growing season and a dearth of transportation meant that people had to make do with what they had. Ingredients were available fresh only briefly. Preserving them as jams, pickles, relishes, cider, maple syrup, and smoked or cured products made them available through the year.

Though the roots of the old ways remain, refrigeration and highways broaden the range and accessibility of foodstuffs today. However, our limited vistas and thickly wooded mountain ranges still suggest isolation—still, there are no major east–west roads to link Vermont and Maine.

In *Migration from Vermont*, published by the Vermont Historical Society several decades ago, Lewis Stilwell points out that more people born in nineteenth-century Vermont lived out of the state than in it. It's another story today as descendants of original Vermont families flock back, bringing with them customs and ideas from other places and adding these new ways to what still exists of the old life in Vermont.

Wonderful Vermont traditions are being integrated with the contemporary these days. As you recognize old favorites here, I hope you will enjoy their gentle, sometimes surprising accommodations to today's tastes.

And, need I say that maple-cured hams, roasted venison, fried green tomatoes, fiddleheads, pies, cider, and strawberry shortcake are as popular today as they were when Vermont was an independent republic.

Through the years a rich heritage has been passed down generation by generation—a strong link that bonds Vermonters to their forebears and the land. *North Country Gourmet* celebrates that legacy and the way it shapes what we serve today.

Vermont's brief growing season relies on short-season and cold-weather crops—vegetables and fruits without exotic-sounding names—simple foods, treasured for what they are. A perfectly ripe ear of Silver Queen corn, picked in the cool of evening, roasted over glowing coals. Crisp russet-skinned apples, pressed into sweet cider or eaten out-of-hand. These foods cannot be improved; the brevity of their season only increases their worth.

The uneven landscape of forested hills and river valleys creates isolated temperature zones. Some plants grown successfully at one end of town don't have a chance at the other end. Oddly, one of the state's most temperate spots borders on Canada—the area referred to as "the islands" in Lake Champlain.

Crops are both hindered and helped by the climate. Late frosts and early snows confine the season to 100 or so days. While the duration and variety of produce is limited, the quality is enhanced. Cold weather prevents the sugar in fruits and vegetables from converting to starch.

The ingredients described in the following chapter are mainly traditional staples of Vermont cooking available at farmers' markets or home gardens throughout this state—and across most of northern North America.

Apples

The world's most cultivated tree fruit, apples grow in all 50 states. Thousands of varieties exist as purposely propagated trees, as natural crosses, or as escaped seedlings. It is convenient to classify them by intended use—as cider, cooking, or dessert varieties. Characteristics for classification include size, shape, color, sugar content, texture, and storage potential.

Apples that ripen in summer do not hold well and must be used soon after harvest. Winter apples can be stored up to 9 months at 32°F or in a controlled atmosphere.

Modern hybrids are less susceptible to disease and biennial cropping than are old-fashioned varieties. Fortunately, treatments exist to control most maladies of the apple. Consequently, nurseries have reintroduced some once-famous, once-vulnerable types.

Newer varieties are bred for freedom from disease, insect resistance, shape, color, and keeping qualities. Though designed for eating out-of-hand, they make fair sauces and passable sweet cider. Because they are bred for high marketability as an all-purpose fruit, their advantages generally benefit only the grower. They bear earlier and heavily and store well. They tend to be bland, nondistinctive, and useless for baking. When you shop for apples, buy with a specific purpose in mind. A pie apple will always make a better pie than will an all-purpose apple.

Wild Apples

True wild apples are the native crabapples that bear tiny sour fruit. They grew throughout North America long before the arrival of European colonists. Crabapples are high in tannin and can be used to improve hard cider if added in small quantities. Old recipes that call for "verjuice" are calling for the fermented juice of crabapples. Extremely dry and tart, verjuice counteracts sweetness when added to sauces in small quantities.

Escaped Apples

Escaped apples grow from the seeds of cultivated apples spread by the elements, birds, animals, or people. Apples grown from seed tend to revert back to the traits of their ancestors—crabapples. No two are exactly alike; using them brings unpredictable results. Since they resemble crabapples, they are useful in cider, jellies, butter, and conserves.

Cider Apples

Cider is the pressed, unfiltered, unpasteurized juice of the apple. It can be enjoyed directly from the apple press or heated with spices as mulled cider. To make mulled cider: add 1 stick cinnamon, 6 cloves, and 6 allspice berries to a quart of cider. Warm over medium-low heat until steaming. It should not boil—this causes the solids to precipitate out of the cider. Serve mugs of mulled cider from the first frosts of September till the spring thaw.

Sweet cider is freshly pressed and unfermented juice; hard cider is fermented and aged juice. Somewhere between them is "fizzy cider"—sweet cider that has begun to ferment of its own accord, usually when it is stored too long. The fizz develops through the action of natural yeasts. The result is pleasantly tart and is commonly used for cooking. Cider is available bottled as sweet, hard, or a nonalcoholic sparkling beverage.

Dessert Apples

These fruits can be enjoyed out-of-hand directly from the tree. Dessert apples can be sweet, tart, soft, hard, crisp, thin-skinned, russeted, juicy. Only dry, mealy, or astringent apples are excluded from this list.

Baking Apples

Apples that retain their shape when baked whole or sliced are usually called pie apples or bakers. Generally, they are tart, well-flavored, and firm.

Sauce Apples

Apples that get soft or mushy when cooked are used for sauces, jelly, and butter. Baking apples tend to produce a sauce that is coarse, dry, or grainy. McIntosh is a good example of an apple that disintegrates when cooked. This trait is bred into some old-fashioned varieties to produce a smooth, buttery sauce. The Peach apple can be made into a silky apple butter the color of fancy-grade maple syrup.

The following guide to apple varieties takes into account what is available from northern wayside produce markets and includes apples grown outside the region.

Summer Apples

Variety	Color/Size	Use	Remarks
Duchess (Oldenberg)	Greenish yellow with red stripes; medium to large	Baking, cider	Firm, fine-grained, juicy, aromatic; superior pie apple. Late summer–early autumn
Famuese (Snow Apple)	Red and yellow with stripes; medium	Dessert, sauce, cider	White, fine-grained flesh; tender, juicy; excellent dessert. Forerunner of the MacIntosh
Lodi	Yellow; large	Sauce, cider	Fine-grained and juicy with a mild flavor
Peach	Yellow with slight red blush; medium	Dessert, sauce	Tender, fine-grained, juicy. Makes a light-colored smooth apple butter. Late summer–early autumn
Red Astrachan	Greenish with red stripes, blue bloom; medium	Baking (pre-ripe), dessert (ripe)	Fine-grained, juicy, aromatic, slightly astringent. Small % of juice improves a bland cider
Yellow Transparent	Pale yellow, medium	Sauce, dessert, cider	Fine-grained, juicy, soft, pleasant flavor

Autumn Apples

Variety	Color/Size	Use	Remarks
Alexander	Red or striped, very large	Baking, cider	Juicy; coarse texture
Chenango Strawberry	Yellowish with red stripes, large	Dessert, sauce	Tender, juicy, aromatic. Early autumn
Cox's Orange Pippin	Mottled orange-red, medium	Dessert, cider	Crisp, very juicy, aromatic, rich flavor. High quality dessert, flavorful cider
Dolgo Crabapple	Red, oblong fruits, small	Apple butter, pickles, jelly, cider	Beautiful flowering landscape tree. Improves bland cider, colors it with crimson nectar
Dudley	Pale yellow with red striped blush, large	Baking	Juicy, aromatic, tender; very good baking
Gravenstein	Yellow with light and dark red stripes, medium to large	Baking, dessert, cider	Firm, juicy, aromatic

Autumn Apples (*continued*)

Variety	Color/Size	Use	Remarks
Maiden Blush	Pale yellow with red blush, medium to large	Baking, drying	Fine-grained, very juicy, tender
McIntosh	Red, striped and washed with green; medium to large	Dessert, sauce, cider	Firm, fine-grained, crisp, aromatic, very good dessert. Late autumn
Northwestern Greening	Yellow or greenish, large	Baking	Medium texture, juicy, slight aroma. Late autumn
Rhode Island Greening	Grass-green to yellowish, medium to very large	Baking, dessert, cider	Yellowish, fine-grained, juicy, rich flesh, unusual flavor, good keeper. Very good baking. Late autumn.
St. Lawrence	Pale yellow with red stripes, medium to large	Dessert, sauce	Fine-grained, tender, juicy, mild flavor
Summer Pearmain	Red striped with darker red, medium	Dessert, baking	Fine, melting, juicy flesh; aromatic
Tompkins King	Red over yellow with russet dots, very large	Dessert, baking	Yellowish, coarse flesh; juicy, aromatic. Late autumn
Westfield (Seek-No-Further)	Red striped with dots, medium	Dessert, cider	Flesh tinged with yellow; rich, aromatic, sometimes a little astringent. Late autumn
Winesap	Various shades of red striped and blotched over a yellow ground, medium	Dessert, cider	Coarse flesh tinged with yellow, very juicy. Late autumn
Wolf River	Red stripes over yellowish ground, very large	Baking	Coarse, tender, dry flesh

Winter Apples

Variety	Color/Size	Use	Remarks
Baldwin	Bright red, large	Baking, dessert	Tender, juicy. Once the most widely propagated apple in the northeast
Bullock	Light yellow with russeting, small to medium	Dessert, cider	Very tender, juicy, and aromatic. Especially esteemed for cider

Variety	Color/Size	Use	Remarks
Cortland	Red with blue cast, medium to large	Dessert, baking, cider	Fine-grained, juicy, discolors slowly when cut. Produces pink cider
Empire	Red, medium to large	Dessert, sauce, cider, baking	Fine-grained, crisp, juicy. High quality dessert; good sauce, cider; fair pie
Golden Delicious	Clear yellow, large	Dessert, baking	Crisp, juicy, sweet, superior dessert
Golden Russet	Yellow-bronze russet, small	Cider, dessert	Fine-grained, tart, crisp, aromatic. Keeps well. Esteemed for cider, good dessert
Granny Smith	Grass-green, large	Baking, dessert	Firm, tart, white flesh discolors slowly
Jonathan	Deep red, small to medium	Baking, cider, dessert	Fine-grained, tart, crisp, juicy, aromatic
Liberty	Deep red, medium	Dessert, sauce, cider	Fine-grained, juicy, aromatic. A virtually disease-free tree
Macoun	Red with blue blush, medium	Dessert, sauce, cider	Crisp, white flesh; aromatic with pleasant flavor
Milwaukee	Yellow with red stripes, large	Baking, cider	Coarse-grained, tender, juicy
Newton	Greenish or yellow, medium to very large	Dessert, cider	Flesh tinged with skin color; tart crisp, juicy, aromatic. Popular dessert, good cider.
Northern Spy	Red stripes over a pale yellow ground, large	Dessert, cider, sauce	Fine-grained, tender, juicy, aromatic
Pumpkin Sweet (Pound Sweet)	Yellow with greenish marbling, very large	Baking	Coarse, sweet flesh with unusual flavor, very good baking. Early winter
Red Delicious	Dark red, conical, large	Dessert, cider	Crisp, sweet, aromatic. Popular dessert; blending base for cider
Rome Beauty	Red mingled with yellow, large	Baking, cider	Dry, coarse texture, aromatic
Roxbury Russet	Greenish or yellowish-brown russet, medium to large	Dessert, cider	Coarse, juicy, aromatic. Over 300-year-old variety
Scott Winter	Red with darker red mottling, small to medium	Baking, dessert	Flesh slightly yellow, sometimes stained with red. Tart, crisp, juicy. Baking early, dessert when milder at end of season.

Variety	Color/Size	Use	Remarks
Smokehouse	Red and greenish yellow, medium to large	Dessert	Crisp, juicy, aromatic, and pleasantly flavored
Spitzenburg	Bright red with yellow dots, medium to large	Dessert, cider	Firm, juicy, aromatic
Stayman Winesap	Greenish-yellow mottled and striped with red, medium to large	Dessert, baking, cider	Flesh tinged with yellow, firm, juicy, aromatic
Tolman Sweet	Clear pale yellow, small to large	Baking	Hard, dry, sweet
Wealthy	Greenish-yellow striped with bright red, large	Dessert, cider, sauce	White flesh, sometimes stained with red; tart, very juicy, fine-grained, crisp.
Winter Banana	Clear pale yellow with pinkish-red blush, large	Dessert	Coarse, juicy, distinctly aromatic
York Imperial	Greenish-yellow with red stripes and blush, medium to large	Dessert, cider	Flesh is yellowish, coarse, and aromatic. Lopsided fruits

Other Fruits

Blueberries

In 1888 Jackson Dawson said in *American Garden* that "A number of growers in Massachusetts are becoming interested in the cultivation of this plant, and we are on the lookout for large varieties, so we may soon expect to see blueberries as large as cherries."

Blueberries are a surprisingly recent phenomenon. Just 100 years after this article appeared, the cultivated high-bush blueberry is bearing those dreamed-of large fruits. In the process it has completely overshadowed the huckleberry.

There are two basic varieties of blueberries, the low-bush and the high-bush. The low-bush is a scruffy, spreading shrub that seldom grows over a foot high. Its small, finely flavored berries ripen early in the season. It grows on dry, rocky hillsides and along stone walls in direct sun or in semi-shaded areas.

The wild high-bush blueberry is a large upright bush that can exceed 8 feet and occasionally reaches 12 feet or more in height. Its berries are larger than the low-bush but of a similar rich flavor. Many high-bush hybrids have been developed to extend the season from early July to the latter part of September. Some varieties are bred to grow only 2–4 feet tall to reduce winter damage.

Commercially purveyed berries are picked before they are totally ripe to prolong shelf life and to protect them from damage during shipping. This procedure may work well for the grower, but it is woe to the buyer. After turning blue, the berries require at least another week on the bush to achieve their full character. When picking the berries, select those that are deeply colored and yield slightly when squeezed. Unripe berries are bland or tasteless.

Strawberries

These luscious fruits range from the pea-sized wild strawberry to some baseball-like hybrids. Their season peaks in July, when many communities celebrate with strawberry shortcake festivals. Strawberries are now available year-round from New Zealand, Florida, California, Chile, Mexico, and Israel. Though these out-of-season varieties cannot hold a candle to a freshly picked native berry, they can raise your spirits in the dead of winter.

When purchasing strawberries, look for pointed rather than fan-shaped berries, which are likely to be hollow. They should have red shoulders, be firm to the touch but not hard, and have a sweet, ripe smell. Irrigation plays an important role in berry quality. Insufficient water causes the seeds to cluster on the tips or along the sides of the berries, making them unappetizing. If they are overirrigated, as are most commercial ones, the plants absorb the excess liquid and produce berries that are large but tasteless and watery.

The tiny, incredibly delicious wild strawberry is the first to ripen in June. All domesticated varieties descend from this wild forebear with its highly concentrated sweet flavor and heady perfume. Their minute size inhibits the gathering of a large quantity. Consider using them as a garnish or in a liqueur where a small amount goes a long way.

The best way to get wonderful native berries, short of growing them yourself, is from pick-your-own operations—a pleasant way to limit cost and ensure quality.

Raspberries

Born on gracefully arcing canes, the raspberry is the aristocrat of berries. It grows wild along roadsides and stonewalls, in old cellar holes, and is among the first to grow in the burned-out wake of a fire. The four main varieties—red, yellow, purple, and black—have similarities, but each exhibits its own distinct characteristics of flavor, aroma, and texture. Raspberries come into season in June, peak in July, and the "everbearing" varieties yield a second crop in the fall.

When a berry is picked, its core remains on the plant, leaving a hollow fruit. Stripped of supporting structure, raspberries are extremely fragile and should be placed in shallow containers to avoid crushing. They should be used soon after picking or purchase; shelf life is short, and they are susceptible to mold.

Raspberries are an aggregate fruit, each drupelet, or segment, being a seed receptacle. Exercise care when cooking with the berries to prevent grinding the seeds, which can impart a bitter flavor to the finished dish. For pureeing, I prefer a manually operated food mill to a blender or food processor.

Blackberries

Blackberries are thorny brambles, related to raspberries. They prefer to inhabit sunny thickets and pastures. Unlike a raspberry, the core remains attached to the berry after picking, making blackberries slightly less fragile than their hollow relatives. They should be used soon after picking. Because the berries will not ripen once picked, look for fruit that is deeply black, soft, and juicy. Violet-colored berries will be hard, dry, and sour.

Blackberries are very seedy—a pint of berries can contain up to a half cup of seeds, which are brittle and must be treated carefully. Puree blackberries with a manually operated food mill to prevent breaking them. Avoid using a blender or food processor, which will grind the seeds, leaving your puree bitter and sandy.

Plums

These members of the rose family include both prune plums and damsons of European and Japanese varieties. Plums may be eaten out-of-hand or canned. Prunes are produced from plums with a high sugar content so they can be dried without fermentation around the pit. When eaten fresh, they are plums; when dried, they are called prunes.

Damsons, a type of plum, are round in shape and can be tart or sour. They are used for pies, preserves, game sauces, cobblers, and pudding cakes. Prune plums are to damsons as sweet cherries are to pie cherries.

Both prune plums and damsons are usually skinned but not cooked before using in recipes. Pureed raw plums are used in ice creams, sherbets, chilled summer soups, and summer drinks. When purchasing plums, look for fruit that is soft yet resilient to the touch. There should be no discoloration at the stem end. The fruit should have the deep, penetrating smell of ripeness.

Cherries

The two main varieties of cherry trees are the tall, stately sweet cherry and the shorter, fan-like sour cherry. Large and heart-shaped, the sweet cherry can range in color from yellow to almost black. Low in acid, it can be eaten out-of-hand or canned. When you buy them at the market, look for cherries that are barely firm and that will spring back when squeezed between the fingers. Avoid fruits that are discolored, that have tightly clinging stems—a sign of immaturity—or that do not smell like well-ripened fruit.

The sour cherry accounts for more than half the total U.S. production of cherries. Most of this crop is frozen or canned. The fruit is smaller, usually clear red in color and high in acid. Sour cherries can be eaten fresh when quite ripe; but, for the most part, they are used in pies, jams, and cooking. The trees are winter hardy and popular in colder climates, where sweet cherries do not fare well.

Pears

One of the most important deciduous fruit trees in the world, the pear ranks second internationally, outproduced only by the apple; it is third in the U.S., behind apples and peaches. A pome fruit, it is similar to the apple in many respects though it is generally sweeter with a softer texture. The fruits range from the robin's-egg size, but uncommonly sweet, Sekel to the huge Williams of France. Some varieties are round or apple-shaped like the Nova, but most are narrow at the stem end and broad in the beam.

Unlike apples, pears contain grit cells that can make the flesh sandy in texture. This condition occurs in some home orchard varieties or in pears that have been stored improperly, picked too late, or cooked when unripe.

Most fruit should be tree-ripened for maximum flavor. Not so pears! Most varieties must be picked while still hard, put into cool, dry storage, and ripened at room temperature. Otherwise, the pears become soft and mealy.

When used in cooking, pears must be treated like apples. This means the fruit should be peeled, cored, and cooked before using in a sherbet, sauce, or similar preparation where a puree is required. An acid ingredient, such as lemon juice, should be employed to prevent discoloration and to heighten flavor. In addition to use in sweet dishes, pears lend themselves to savory preparations, especially veal, duckling, hare, pork, cheese, and in salads of bitter greens.

A good test for ripeness is to pull on the stem. If the stem pulls out with just the barest resistance, the pear is perfectly ripe.

Peaches

The peach is the second most popular tree fruit in the United States, surpassed only by the apple. Peaches occur as freestone, the flesh easily removed from the pit, or clingstone, where the flesh clings tenaciously to the stone. They range in color from creamy white to yellow, right up to bright red. A drupe fruit, the seed is contained in a hard casing surrounded by the edible flesh and the skin. The skin and stone must be removed before proceeding with a recipe.

To skin peaches, bring a large pot of water to a boil, plunge the peaches into it a few at a time so the water continues to boil. Leave the fruit in the boiling water for 15–20 seconds, remove with a slotted spoon, and immerse in ice water. The skins can now be easily slipped from the fruits, which are cut in half and the stones removed. Many varieties of peach oxidize when the flesh is exposed to the air and turn an unappealing brown. Squeeze lemon juice over the prepared fruit to prevent discoloration.

Peaches are extremely versatile—use them with meat and in desserts, preserves, and relishes. Ham, pork, duckling, veal, shellfish, cheese, and salads are complemented by their smooth, sweet tang. When purchasing them, you should be able to smell them before you even pick one up. Peaches should yield slightly under pressure and be free of spots, bruises, and mold. Once ripened, they have a short shelf life and require immediate attention or they will be lost. They do not store well; out-of-season fruits are tasteless and mealy. Fruits canned or frozen in season are always better than storage fruit or peaches grown in the Southern Hemisphere.

Cranberries

The low, creeping American cranberry thrives in low-lying areas of southern New England. A relative of the blueberry, it ranges in color from pink to deep red or mottled. The berries are acid and cannot be eaten out-of-hand. When cooked with sugar, they retain a snappy quality. Relish or sauce made from cranberries is a regular accompaniment at holiday feasts.

Cranberries are an autumnal fruit; harvesting continues until late October. They combine well with apples and pears for sauces, pies, juice, and wine. When purchasing cranberries, look for berries that are firm and richly colored. Pick through them to remove stones, stems, leaves, and inferior berries.

A related fruit, the mountain cranberry, is not a true cranberry even though the two are members of the genus *Vaccinium*. Despite the differences, mountain cranberries can be substituted in recipes calling for cranberries. The flavor of mountain cranberries is a combination of cranberries, blueberries, and currants. They contain their own pectin so they are popular additions to jellies, conserves, and chilled sauces.

Rhubarb

Classified as a vegetable, rhubarb is treated like a fruit as its alternate name, "pie-plant," attests. A hardy, long-lived perennial, its long, reddish, succulent leafstalks are wonderful in pies, cobblers, compotes, and preserves. It requires a cool climate, one in which the ground freezes, and is similar in culture to asparagus.

The stalks appear early in the growing season and can be harvested throughout the summer. The leaves contain oxalic acid, which is used commercially for dying and bleaching. The leaves are mildly poisonous and should not be eaten.

Little preparation is required. Just peel the outer, fiberous layer to expose the juicy interior of the stalk (freshly cut, tender young stalks need not be peeled, however). When you buy rhubarb, look for firm, glossy stalks that snap if bent to expose a moist, aromatic interior.

Winter Squashes

This is another type of vegetable that I feel compelled to include in this section on fruits. A traditional storage crop, winter squashes serve as the basis for many desserts and baked goods. Grown on expansive vines, squashes require a lot of space in a sunny, well-drained spot. Their lively, multicolored shapes contrast brilliantly with the bare ground and provide a romantic aspect to an autumn landscape.

Sweet, smooth-textured squashes are required for desserts when a grainy or flaky consistency would have an unfavorable effect. Soufflés, cheesecakes, pies, ice creams, and puddings demand the smooth, even puree supplied by butternut and buttercup squashes, sugar pumpkin, and pie pumpkin. When a grainy texture would go unnoticed in breads, cookies, coffeecakes, or the like, other varieties can be used. Smaller squashes can be baked whole and then pulped, scooped out, and pureed. Larger ones can be cut up and steamed. They should be well drained of any cooking liquid before proceeding with a recipe.

Herbs

Herbs continue to intrigue us. Early books deal with their medical, culinary, and domestic applications. Before refrigeration, herbs were used in cooking to mask spoilage. Today we use them to subtly enhance the flavor of fresh foods.

Herbs stir the senses, provide culinary variety, and are a delight to grow and use. Fresh herbs are preferable to the dried ones. When substituting, use one tablespoon of chopped, fresh herbs to one teaspoon of dried, a 3:1 ratio.

Herbs can be preserved for cold-weather use by freezing, drying, or processing into herbal oils and vinegars. Flavored oils and vinegars are easy to make. Place several sprays of a chosen herb in a bottle of the liquid. Seal and place in a warm, sunny spot for 3 days to a week to develop the esters. Strain the liquid into bottles that can be tightly sealed. Garnish with a single branchlet of the herb for visual reference, and use as needed.

Basil

A tomato salad dressed with the clovelike taste of chopped fresh basil always makes me think of warm summer days. Harvest basil before it flowers, chop coarsely with a knife, mix with olive oil, and store in your freezer for a year-round supply. Never use a food processor to chop basil. The machine bruises the leaves, expresses the flavorful oil, and greatly diminishes the flavor. Basil is useful with pasta, tomatoes, chicken, veal, and in salad dressing.

Sage

Sage, a winter-hardy perennial, makes a beautiful border of accent planting in a rock garden. The silver leaves and blue flowers last well into autumn. Its flavor intensifies, for the better, when the herb is dried. Use the chopped fresh or dried leaves with turkey or chicken, in biscuits, with cheddar cheese and poultry stuffing, and as the primary seasoning in pork sausage. Rubbed sage is the same as ground sage. The term goes back to the time when the herb was rubbed through the fingers to make it a powder.

Thyme

An important culinary herb, there are endless creeping and bushlike varieties, all of which have different flavors and scents. The most common variety lends its distinctive peppery flavor to almost any preparation. When fresh it has a mint or clovelike quality and should be used sparingly.

Tarragon

Fresh tarragon has a distinctive licorice aroma and taste. Dried tarragon is quite different from fresh. Don't use tarragon in combination with assertive herbs but allow it to reveal its own character. Tarragon works as well with strongly flavored game and beef as it does with poultry, veal, and fish. Add the herb according to the strength of the flavor it is to enhance.

Chives

This prolific perennial is a member of the lily family and is related to the onion. It is not unusual to see the tender green shoots pushing through the snow on a warm spring day. Use chopped, fresh chives with white meats, vegetables, cheese, in salad dressing, and breads. Crunchy and garliclike in flavor, the lavender blooms make an attractive garnish and look beautiful in a tossed green salad.

Parsley

A simply sauteed trout or breast of chicken requires little else to complete the dish except a touch of lemon juice and some chopped parsley. Parsley's clean, fresh taste enlivens anything it touches. It is useful in soups, salads, stocks, sauces, and in conjunction with other herbs. Since it is available year-round at supermarkets, there is no point in drying parsley; but, if you have a nice crop, it will freeze well if dried in a spinner and chopped.

Savory

Summer savory, an annual herb, grows abundantly in any well-drained sunny spot. Winter savory is a slow-growing, woody perennial adaptable to almost any growing condition. Winter savory is spicier than the annual variety but is interchangeable where savory is required. Known as the bean herb, its thymelike flavor enhances any dried legume or fresh bean as well as aiding in the digestion of legumes. Use savory in stuffings and soups and with pork, turkey, and cheese.

Dill

Chopped fresh dill is delicate and should be added, without cooking, as the final ingredient of a soup or sauce. Use the flowery tops in pickling cucumbers, beets, green beans, green tomatoes, and asparagus. New potatoes, peas, poached salmon, and cucumber salad are all improved by its distinctive fragrance.

Fresh dill is available at the market. Although your own crop can be dried successfully, it is best preserved by rolling finger-width packets of the fronds in plastic wrap and storing them in your freezer. Chop the dill as needed and add it directly to your recipe.

Mint

Easily identified by its square stem, mint comes in hundreds of varieties, spearmint and peppermint being the best known. It takes over quickly in any garden so you must take steps to isolate it from the rest of your herbs. Mint is particularly compatible with sweet foods. Try it with sliced fresh fruit, apple pie, chocolate, sherbet, and iced tea.

When cooking with mint, add it at the end of the cooking to retain the fresh flavor. Serve mint jelly or sauce with venison and lamb, or add chopped mint leaves to peas, carrots, turnips, and parsnips.

Bay

Bay is available as whole dried leaves or in powdered form. Most cookbooks warn against using too many bay leaves and consequently don't use enough. Powdered bay, however, should be used sparingly. Bay is invaluable for pâtés, soups, stocks, sauces, and marinades.

Rosemary

An evergreen shrub with deep green, aromatic needlelike leaves, rosemary grows to a height of 2–3 feet. Roasts absorb its piney, resinous flavor when the branches are simply laid on the meat or in the cavity of poultry. Rosemary makes a beautiful houseplant but requires daily attention to keep the thirsty needles and roots moist. It does, however, pay for its keep.

The dried leaves are tough, even after cooking, and must be pulverized before using. Use this fragrant herb in stews, especially lamb and venison, and with winter vegetables. Lay rosemary branches on the glowing coals of a barbeque to flavor grilled fish and meats with its fragrant smoke.

Oregano and Marjoram

For culinary purposes these herbs are almost interchangeable. Oregano is a hardy perennial that spreads rapidly. Marjoram, although a perennial in warmer climates, must be treated as an annual in the North Country. Both herbs tend to become more concentrated and complex in flavor when dried. Of the two, marjoram is able to hold up better in cooking when used fresh. Used most frequently to season tomato sauce and pizza, both oregano and marjoram can also be combined with chicken, turkey, veal, and pork.

Dandelion

Pick young dandelion greens before the plant flowers. After blooming the leaves become bitter. Dandelion is rich in vitamins A and C.

Sorrel

In its wild form this is the common pasture weed known as sourgrass. The larger and more tender leaves of the cultivated variety, French sorrel, is the green that most frequently finds its way into the kitchen. Its lemony and pleasantly sour leaves are used in sorrel soup, with fish, in salads, and in omelets. It is rich in vitamins A and C.

Garlic

Garlic is high in vitamins and protein. It reduces blood pressure, and it aids in digestion. Flavor depends on preparation. It is most potent if smashed with the flat side of a knife or aerated, raw, through a garlic press and added at the end of the cooking. It can be boiled to make it mild, roasted to a nutlike flavor, or sauteed for a sharp, spicy taste. Most garlic lovers would agree that there is nothing that can't be improved by the addition of garlic.

Spruce

A tall, spire-shaped evergreen, spruce grows throughout the northern United States and Canada. The fresh green needles on the branch tips have a heady, resinous fragrance that is very appealing with cured fish, vegetables, and woodland game. Roast ruffed grouse, young wild turkey, and pheasant on a bed of spruce, making a pan sauce from the drippings. Steam or bake root vegetables with spruce boughs or include branch tips in a marinade for venison and bear.

Other Products

Milk and Cream

The dairy products we buy are by law pasteurized. Commercial milk products undergo a second processing called homogenization. The fat particles are broken down into small droplets and evenly distributed throughout the product in a permanent emulsion.

The standards for grading milk products are set by the U.S. Department of Agriculture, which regulates the percentage of butterfat in each product as follows:

Heavy cream	36–40%
Medium cream	30–35%
Light cream	18%
Half and half	12%
Whole milk	3.25%
Lowfat milk	1% or 2%
Skim milk	All the butterfat removed

It should go without saying that all milk products need to be kept refrigerated and used before the date stamped on the container. The fresher the milk, the better it will be, in flavor and nutrition. Milk starts to break down before it reaches the expiration date. You may have noticed this if you have tried to make a white sauce that breaks down as soon as the mixture reaches a boil. The problem was that the milk just wasn't very fresh. It is a good habit to smell milk every time you remove the cap. It is much worse to find out after you have poured it into your coffee.

Cultured Dairy Products

The addition of favorable bacteria to various milk products creates a whole new range of foods. Bacteria ferment the lactose into lactic acid and cause the milk or cream to thicken and to develop a smooth texture and pleasantly sour flavor. The following products are paired with their respective derivatives:

> Crème fraiche from heavy cream
> Sour cream from light cream
> Yogurt from whole milk
> Buttermilk from skim milk. When buttermilk is the byproduct of making butter, it is known as churned buttermilk. Its use is beneficial in baked goods.

It is simple to make your own cultured products. As it is almost impossible to find crème fraiche in the market, making your own is the only way to have it. Pour a given amount of cream, milk, or skim milk into a stainless steel bowl and add a little of a cultured product to it—it doesn't seem to matter if you use yogurt, sour cream, or buttermilk. Stir the mixture to distribute the cultured product throughout. Cover tightly and place in a spot that maintains a 90°F temperature for 24 hours. I have used the top of a refrigerator to draw the heat from the motor and also the back section of a griddle that has a pilot light in the front. When the mixture has thickened, pour it into a container, cover, and refrigerate. It will be ready to use when chilled and set.

Butter

Butter is made by separating the fat from the whey of cream. Commercially it is sold as either sweet butter, which originally meant that it had been made from sweet rather than sour cream but has now come to mean unsalted, or salted butter. Salted butter has a longer refrigerator life, the salt acting as its preservative, but it tends to be watery and can contain up to 2 tablespoons of salt per pound. I use only unsalted butter, adding salt if it is required in the amount deemed necessary. Unsalted butter spoils quickly and should be kept frozen until you wish to use it to preserve its sweet, fresh taste. It is unsurpassed as a table spread and for baking and cooking.

Cheddar Cheese

Next to maple syrup, Cheddar cheese is the product for which Vermont is best known. It is a semihard, yellowish (never orange) cheese that is named after a town in England, where it has been made since the sixteenth century. Its name comes from a step in the product's manufacture. The process of cutting the fused curd into slabs and stacking them has come to be known as "cheddaring." It is undoubtedly the single most popular cheese in the world.

Historically Vermont has been dependent on dairying, and there has always been a great deal of milk on hand that has required immediate attention. Before refrigeration, this was an even greater problem, and manufacturing the milk into cheese was the perfect solution. Cheese production took place in the warmer months of the year when butter could not be made in quantity because of spoilage. The raw product, once processed into cheese, could be kept for as long as 2 years.

Cheddar is sold according to its age, the ripeness causing it to be either mild, sharp, or extra-sharp. Cheese that is 2–6 months old is sold as mild. It is useful for baking and light sauces where less tang is warranted. Cheddar that is 6–12 months old is known as sharp. It is popular as a table and all-purpose cheese. Beyond a year old the cheese is extra-sharp and is exactly that. It may still be used on the table or in cooking, but generally in reduced quantities because of its pungent character.

When purchasing Cheddar, look for an even coloring and consistency and a fine aroma. It should be just slightly crumbling, smooth, with a hint of dryness. If it smells "skunky," it has been improperly stored and is probably rancid. An unusually crumbly cheese has undoubtedly been frozen; while still edible, such cheddar cheese is not worthy of purchase.

Eggs

In northern New England people will pay extra to get eggs with brown shells. On the other hand, McDonald's will not purchase brown eggs. There is no difference in taste between an egg with a white and one with a brown, pink, or blue shell. A high-quality egg is one in which the yolk is dead center in the white, the white has a thick consistency, and there is little airspace between the egg and the shell. They are classed according to weight as indicated in the size-weight chart on the following page.

Size	Weight (oz/dozen)
Jumbo	30
Extra large	27
Large	24
Medium	21
Small	18
Peewee (pullet)	15

All recipes in this book call for large eggs, which weigh a convenient 2 ounces apiece. Like anything else, eggs should be as fresh as possible. They should be kept refrigerated when not in use. Cooked foods containing eggs should be refrigerated if not eaten the day they are made. Hollandaise sauce should be eaten immediately. It will not keep and should be discarded if not entirely used.

Recently there have been warnings against the consumption of raw or lightly cooked eggs because of the danger of contamination by salmonella, a bacteria causing food poisoning. The American Egg Board maintains that healthy individuals incur a very minor risk of contracting food poisoning. The board recommends, however, that egg dishes for pregnant women, very young children, the elderly, and individuals with medical problems (especially those affecting the immune system) be thoroughly cooked. Raw eggs should be used only in foods intended for immediate use, or that will be promptly refrigerated or frozen, and in salad dressings with a high acid content. For further information, contact the American Egg Board, 1460 Renaissance Drive, Park Ridge, Illinois 60068. The board publishes an informative booklet entitled *Eggcyclopedia*, plus pamphlets on such subjects as eggs and salmonella and egg handling and care.

Egg shells contain between 6,000 and 8,000 tiny pores. These allow the egg to "breathe." An old French recipe calls for eggs to be stored overnight with truffles—the eggs absorbing the heady aroma—and made into an omelet the next day. Eggs will also absorb unwanted smells and should be stored in a clean refrigerator in their carton rather than in the egg nests provided in some refrigerators.

When hard-cooking eggs, add a couple of tablespoons of vinegar to the water. Acids and proteins are enemies. The vinegar will seep through the pores of the shell and cause the white of the egg to contract away from the shell. This greatly simplifies shell removal.

Maple Syrup

When winter breaks under the heat of the northward-climbing sun, it is time for sugaring. The sap begins to rise in the maples; and though the wet snow continues to pile up, the smell and feel of spring hangs heavily in the air. It is during this period of freezing nights and warm days that sugar makers ply their trade.

Town Meeting Day, the first Tuesday in March, usually signals the beginning of the season in Vermont. Buckets are hung or pipelines strung to collect the sap. It is this early run sap that is boiled down to make the lightest and fanciest grade of syrup. Collecting and boiling continues until the buds begin to swell and the sap becomes milky.

The flavor of syrup differs because of the time of the season it is gathered, the differences among trees, the exposure of a particular "sugarbush" (adjacent trees in the same area), the handling, the length of time between collection and boiling, the speed of the boiling procedure, and the cleanliness of the operation.

Sap averages 2–3 percent sugar content. It requires about 40 gallons to make a single gallon of syrup. Still a cottage industry, syrup production is much the same as it was two centuries ago. Though wooden buckets have been replaced by galvanized metal ones and plastic pipelines and iron boiling kettles and pans have yielded to the evaporator, syrup production is still traditional and labor-intensive.

The brick-lined "arch" is stoked with soft wood to fire the evaporator. When the sap has been boiled to a concentrated form, it is tested to comply with state and federal standards. The syrup is ready when it reaches 219°F, discounting one degree for each 550 feet above sea level, and scales out to 11 pounds per gallon. The finished product is 31 percent water, 67 percent sucrose, 1 percent malic acid, and 1 percent invert sugar.

The flavor of syrup ranges from the delicate lightness of fancy to the caramel pungency of commercial grades. The grading system changed somewhat during the 1980s. During that period the federal government decided it was time to standardize a century-old grading process. The syrup is now classed by color with all grades except commercial, called grade A.

Grade A Light Amber, also known as Vermont Fancy, is made from the early run sap. It is very pale in color with a delicate aroma and taste that is greatly appreciated by connoisseurs. It is best used for sugar-on-snow, on breakfast cakes, on ice cream, or in hot or cold beverages.

Grade A Medium Amber (formerly Grade A) is a good middle-of-the-road syrup. It has a more intense maple flavor than Fancy while still retaining some delicacy. It is useful as an all-purpose syrup and can be used for cooking if you do not have a lesser grade on hand.

Grade A Dark Amber (formerly Grade B) is rich, deeply flavored, and has a color that is similar to strong tea. It is useful in baked beans, for glazing meats, and in sauces, breads, desserts, custards, pickles, and other pre-served foods.

Vermont Grade B (about half-way between old Grades B and C) is as dark as molasses and has a pronounced smoky flavor. Generally sold in bulk, it is still useful for cooking, a little going a very long way. This is the product used by large manufacturers, adding about 2 percent, to flavor corn syrup breakfast dressings.

Maple sugars range from a soft spread called maple butter, which looks like slightly granulated honey, through many variants to hard-cake sugar. A gallon of maple syrup, weighing 11 pounds, will produce about 8 pounds of light brown, translucent sugar. Before World War II almost all sap was boiled down into sugar, with syrup being the rarity. Now the reverse is true, with most of the sugar produced becoming those wonderful maple leaf-shaped candies. A new product called maple crystals (granulated maple sugar) is gaining popularity and is turning up in little packets on restaurant tables to be added to coffee and tea.

Common Crackers

The Cross brothers, of Montpelier, Vermont, first made this cracker in 1828. A barrel containing 1,200 crackers was considered a year's supply for a family. Once the mainstay of country stores, the cracker barrel has become a symbol of rural America.

Common crackers are yeast-raised, made with wheat flour, potato flakes, and shortening. Baked in molds, 1¾ inches across and ¾ inch thick, the flaky rounds are usually eaten split in two, toasted, and buttered. They are the traditional accompaniment to Cheddar cheese. An old recipe for "cracker puffs" calls for soaking the crackers in ice water for a few minutes, letting them dry, buttering the tops, arranging on a sheet pan, and baking in a hot oven for a few minutes till puffed and golden.

Crackers and other products may be ordered from: The Vermont Country Store, P.O. Box 1108, Manchester Center, Vermont 05255-1108.

Stocks and Soups

✦

Brown Stock

Chicken Stock

Bisque of Salmon with Peas

Zucchini Bisque

Corn and Parsnip Chowder

Broccoli Cheddar Soup

Tomato Basil Soup

Sausage and Apple Soup

Split-Pea Soup with Smoked Meat

Dilled Cauliflower and Carrot Soup

Baked Onion Soup with Melted Cheddar and Bacon

Homemade soups are wholesome, everyday fare—one-dish meals that satisfy the senses with their essential qualities: colorful mosaics of vegetables, steaming aromas, and deep flavors. Their basis can be beef bones, chicken carcasses, and vegetable trimmings, ingredients thought unfit for other methods of preparation. These leftovers are often relegated to the soup kettle with no intention other than gaining one more meal. Yet, these are the components which contain the richest flavors and highest nutritional value.

The preparation of soups is relative to their composite ingredients. Vegetable soups require a brief cooking time to retain inherent colors, textures, vitamin content, and flavors. Soups made with fish are cooked just to the point where the meat is opaque and flaky; often the fish is added near the end of the preparation. Soups made from fowl are cooked only until the meat is tender. Overcooking produces a dry, stringy result—-1½ hours is enough to tenderize the toughest old bird; younger birds seldom require more than 45 minutes. Preparations utilizing red meats are calculated according to the cut of meat. The tougher pieces, such as shanks, bottom round, chuck, neck meat, and "soup bones," need up to 3 hours of slow simmering to tenderize.

Vegetables, with the exception of flavoring agents like garlic, onions, carrots, and celery, should not be added to long-simmering soups. Potatoes, corn, peas, broccoli, asparagus, and similar vegetables, used to garnish the soup, should be added near the end of the cooking and simmered only until tender.

The acidic nature of some vegetables can react with iron pots, producing an off-taste. Onions and tomatoes, if used in quantity as in onion soup or tomato bisque, should not be prepared in an iron pot. Wine and vinegar will also cause this effect with iron.

Homemade soups call for little accompaniment. A basket of steaming biscuits, wedges of johnnycake, warmed breadsticks, sliced hearty bread, or toasted common crackers served with sweet butter round out the meal perfectly (see Chapter 8, Breads and Breakfast Cakes, and Chapter 1, section Other Products: Common Crackers).

Homemade Stocks

Making stocks at home is often overlooked. A quick commercial base or canned broth seems easier. These products are certainly convenient, but generally lend little more to a recipe than coloring. They are always high in sodium. Homemade stocks are just as easy to use, once they have been prepared, which need be only a few times a year. Most importantly, they are economical to make, very nutritious, salt-free, and they have a flavor, aroma, and richness that cannot be approached by any commercial product.

You will probably want to place your 5-gallon pot where you plan to let it simmer, before filling it, because of its weight when full. Never cover the pot while a stock is simmering. The premise that the goodness is trapped in the pot is false. Covering the pot will cause the fats and soluble proteins to emulsify, rendering the stock cloudy and bitter.

You should be able to see the stock moving in the pot but never actively boiling. This operation is well suited to the tops of wood-fired heating stoves as well as wood cookstoves. The long, slow burn will keep the stock simmering without adding to your gas or electric bills.

Once you have made the stock, portion it for later use in conveniently sized freezer containers. Use ice cube trays to freeze stock for sauces and pint containers for soups and stews.

Brown Stock
Yield 1 gallon

Save beef or veal bones, trimmings, and chicken or pheasant carcasses in your freezer. Brown stock benefits from the addition of lightly flavored fowl, which sweetens it and adds depth to the flavor. When you have accumulated a sufficient quantity of bones, you will probably be ready to make a batch of stock.

Substitute venison or moose bones for a game stock. Lamb bones should be used only for stocks used in lamb recipes. Lamb has an assertive flavor that does not lend itself to other meats.

(Continued)

About 8 lb meaty beef or veal bones, trimmings, and a chicken carcass
   or two
¼ cup vegetable oil
1 lb carrots, unpeeled and chopped coarse
1 ½ lb onions, unpeeled and chopped coarse
4 stalks celery, sliced
2 bay leaves
Handful fresh parsley
1 tsp whole black peppercorns
1 tsp leaf thyme
4 cloves garlic
2 lb tomatoes chopped
Cold water to deglaze roasting pan and to fill 5-gallon pot

✦ Saw the bones, or break them up with a cleaver, into pieces smaller
than your fist. Arrange these pieces in a single layer in a roasting pan
with any trimmings or fowl carcasses. Drizzle vegetable oil over the
bones so they are well coated. Place the pan in a preheated 450°F oven
and roast for 45 minutes. Turn the bones halfway through the roasting so
they will brown evenly. Add the onions, carrots, and celery to the roasting pan and stir them together with the bones. Roast a further 45 minutes,
stirring once or twice to promote an even coloring.

Empty the contents of the pan into a 5-gallon pot. A canning kettle suits
this purpose. Pour 1 inch cold water into the roasting pan and place the
pan on a burner set on high flame. Scrape up the browned bits clinging
to the pan and pour into the stockpot. Add the remaining ingredients. Fill
the pot to within an inch of the rim with cold water.

Bring the stock to a boil, then reduce the heat so that the liquid simmers
quite slowly. After an hour or so, skim off the foam and fat that have
accumulated on the surface.

Simmer until the stock is reduced by one-half. Strain into a clean pot
and remove the fat from the surface. Return the strained stock to the
stove and reduce it until you have 1 gallon of rich, fragrant stock. The
entire reduction procedure should take 8–12 hours. Skim the stock, as
necessary, while it simmers. Cool and apportion the stock into conveniently sized freezer containers for future use.

Chicken Stock
Yield 2 gallons

Chicken stock is easier to make than brown stock. You don't have to roast the bones in advance, and the cooking time is much shorter. If you would like to make a brown chicken stock (useful in sauces for game birds), follow the directions for brown stock, substituting chicken bones for the beef. Chicken stock is an extremely versatile cooking medium. It can serve as the vehicle for many vegetable soups and stews as well as for sauces for white meats and small game.

> **About 8 lb chicken carcasses and giblets, excluding hearts and livers**
> **1½ lb onions, unpeeled and chopped coarse**
> **1 lb carrots, unpeeled and chopped coarse**
> **8 stalks celery, sliced**
> **4 cloves garlic**
> **1 tsp whole black peppercorns**
> **2 bay leaves**
> **1 tsp leaf thyme**
> **Juice and zest 1 lemon**
> **Handful fresh parsley**
> **Cold water to fill 5-gallon pot**

✦ Chop the chicken carcasses and place in a 5-gallon pot with the remaining ingredients. A canning kettle suits this purpose. Place the pot where you wish to let it cook and fill it to within an inch of the rim with cold water. Bring to a boil and then reduce the heat until the stock barely bubbles.

After the stock has simmered for 1 hour, skim the foam and fat from the surface. Simmer for a total of 3 hours. Strain the stock into a clean pot and continue to let it cook until reduced to 2 gallons. Skim the surface of the stock as necessary. Cool the stock and apportion it into conveniently sized freezer containers for future use.

Soups

Bisque of Salmon with Peas
Yield 6 meal-size or 10 first-course servings

Yankee frugality yields surprising results in an elegant and richly flavored soup made from the carcass (head and skeleton) and trimmings of
a salmon, left over after the meat has been used for other dishes.

4 Tbsp butter
2 medium onions, peeled and diced
2 stalks celery with leaves, peeled and sliced thin
2 cloves garlic, peeled and sliced
Small handful fresh parsley
2 medium potatoes, peeled and diced
6 cups cold water
1½ cups tomato puree
1 salmon carcass, cut into 4 pieces
1 bay leaf
½ tsp thyme
¼ tsp whole black peppercorns
1 cup garden peas
½ cup heavy cream
¼ cup sherry
Salt and pepper to taste
Fresh, chopped dill for garnish

✦ Melt the butter, over very low heat, in a large pot. Add the onions,
celery, garlic, parsley, and potatoes. Cover and stew until the vegetables
have cooked, without coloring, about 30 minutes. Add the water, tomato
puree, salmon carcass, herbs, and spices. Bring to a boil, then reduce it to
a simmer and cook uncovered for 20 minutes.

Remove the pieces of salmon carcass to a bowl and leave to cool.
Meanwhile, pass the soup through a food mill and then puree it until
very smooth in a blender. This may seem like performing the same task
twice. Actually, the food mill removes any errant fish bones and whole
spices prior to blending.

Return the puree to a clean pot and adjust the consistency by adding water to thin or by reducing over medium heat to thicken. It should have the viscosity of heavy cream. Pick the meat from the carcass and flake apart any large pieces.

Precook fresh peas in a quart of lightly salted water, drain, and cool. Add frozen peas directly to the soup.

Add the cream, sherry, salmon, and peas to the soup, heat just to the boiling point. Season to taste with salt and pepper and serve garnished with chopped fresh dill.

Zucchini Bisque
Yield 8–10 meal-size servings

Pure and simple, the subtle flavor of zucchini permeates this pureed soup. This is a handy way to use those squashes of summer that overtake your garden. Freeze in conveniently sized containers for homemade goodness in a hurry.

¼ lb butter
5 lb zucchini, sliced (about 12 cups)
3 cups onions, sliced
2 cups chicken stock, canned chicken broth, or 2 bouillon cubes in 2 cups water
Salt and pepper to taste
Croutons and grated Parmesan cheese for garnish

✦ Melt the butter over medium-low heat in a large pot. Add the onions and cook, stirring occasionally, until the slices have softened without coloring. Add the zucchini and stir the vegetables together. Cover the pot and stew, stirring occasionally, 15–20 minutes. The zucchini should soften but still retain its bright green color. Puree the mixture in a blender and pour into a clean pot. Thin the puree to the desired consistency with the heated chicken stock. Season to taste with salt and pepper. Serve with freshly grated Parmesan cheese and croutons.

Corn and Parsnip Chowder
Yield 8–10 meal-size servings

Hearty vegetable chowders developed inland are standard winter fare in Vermont. Less well known than creamy New England clam chowder, these satisfying soups substituted parsnips, carrots, turnips, jerusalem artichokes, and corn for the generally unavailable seafood. Serve this one as a one-dish meal with common crackers, rolls, or johnnycake.

8 strips bacon, in ½-inch dice
2 medium onions, small dice
2 stalks celery, small dice
½ tsp leaf thyme
1 bay leaf
Grating fresh nutmeg
Pinch cayenne pepper
3 Tbsp all-purpose flour
2 cups chicken stock, canned chicken broth, or 2 bouillon cubes in
    2 cups water
4 cups milk
1 cup boiling potatoes, peeled, in ¼-inch dice
1 cup parsnips, peeled, in ¼-inch dice
3 cups corn
Salt and pepper to taste

✦ Cook the bacon in a heavy pot, over low heat, until crisp. Remove it with a slotted spoon to a small bowl and reserve. Add the onions, celery, herbs, and spices. Cook until the onions are transparent. Sprinkle the flour over the vegetables and stir to make a paste. Add the chicken stock and scrape the bottom of the pot with a wooden spoon to loosen any bits clinging to it. Pour in the milk and add the potatoes and parsnips. Bring slowly to a boil, then reduce to a simmer. Cook, stirring occasionally, until the potatoes and parsnips are tender, about 10 minutes. Add the corn and simmer until just cooked through, about 2 minutes. Season the soup to taste with salt and pepper, bearing in mind the quantity of salt already present from the bacon.

Garnish individual bowls of the chowder with the reserved bacon. Pass a peppermill at the table.

Broccoli Cheddar Soup
Yield 8–10 meal-size servings

Broccoli, a cold-hardy vegetable, continues to thrive after the frosts come. Once the central head is harvested, an uneven collection of sideshoots follow. This soup uses the odds and ends of the broccoli harvest in a smooth, richly colored bisque enhanced by tangy, sharp Cheddar cheese.

2 Tbsp butter
2 medium onions, sliced thin
Good handful fresh parsley
2 Tbsp all-purpose flour
4 cups chicken stock, canned chicken broth, or 4 bouillon cubes in 4 cups water
4 cups milk
Good pinch cayenne pepper
Grating (pinch) fresh nutmeg
2 lb fresh broccoli, sliced thin; reserve 1 cup small florets for the garnish
½ lb sharp Cheddar cheese, grated (about 2 cups)
2 tsp salt or to taste
½ tsp Worcestershire sauce

✦ Melt the butter, over low heat, in a large pot. Add the onions and parsley, cook until softened. Sprinkle the flour over the onions and stir to a paste. Pour in the stock and the milk and add the spices. Gradually bring to a boil and reduce to a simmer; cook slowly for 10 minutes. Increase the heat, add the broccoli, and cook for 2 minutes. The broccoli should be just softened and still retain its bright green color. Immediately puree the soup in a blender and return it to a clean pot. Set the pot over low heat and gradually stir in the cheese. Do not allow the soup to boil. When the cheese has melted, season to taste with salt and Worcestershire sauce.

While the soup is cooking, blanch the florets in boiling water for a half minute. Plunge them into ice water and reserve. When the soup is ready to be served, drain the florets and stir them into the soup. The small broccoli flowers will provide a crisp counterpart to the smooth bisque.

Tomato Basil Soup
Yield 8–10 meal-size servings

Put your late summer–early autumn bumper crop of tomatoes to work in this fragrant vermillion soup. Keep some in your freezer for a warming midwinter suggestion of summer. Serve with freshly grated Parmesan cheese and garlic bread.

¼ lb salt pork or bacon, rind removed, sliced into thin postage stamp-sized pieces
2 cups onions, sliced thin
4 cloves garlic, peeled and sliced
Small handful fresh parsley
1 Tbsp fresh thyme leaves or 1 tsp dried
2 bay leaves
Pinch cayenne pepper
3 cups zucchini, sliced (about 1 lb)
2 Tbsp all-purpose flour
8 cups tomatoes, peeled, deseeded, and chopped, or 4 lb canned tomatoes packed in juice
2 cups chicken stock, canned chicken broth, or 2 bouillon cubes in 2 cups water
4 Tbsp fresh basil, chopped
Parmesan cheese, grated, for garnish

✦ Fry the salt pork in a large pot over low heat until nicely browned. Remove it with a slotted spoon and reserve. Add the onions, garlic, parsley, thyme, bay leaves, and cayenne. Cook until the onions have softened, stirring occasionally. Add the zucchini and cook until softened. Sprinkle in the flour and stir the mixture together. Add the tomatoes and chicken stock, bring to a boil, and then reduce the heat and simmer it gently for 30 minutes.

Pass the soup through the medium disc of a food mill and return the soup to a clean pot. Add the basil and the reserved salt pork and simmer for an additional 15–20 minutes or until the consistency of the soup is to your liking. Season to taste with salt and pepper, bearing in mind the amount of salt in the pork.

Sausage and Apple Soup
Yield 8–10 servings

This soup combines traditional companions, applesauce and pork, with the snappy flavor of crushed caraway seeds. Hearty and filling, sausage and apple soup is a complete winter meal. Serve with dark bread or hot johnnycake.

6 McIntosh apples, peeled, cored, and sliced
4 medium potatoes, peeled and sliced
1 medium onion, peeled and sliced thin
2 cloves garlic, peeled and sliced
1 stalk celery, peeled and sliced thin
½ lb bulk pork sausage
One 12-oz bottle beer or ale
4 cups chicken stock, canned chicken broth, or 4 bouillon cubes in 4 cups water
½ tsp ground savory
2 tsp caraway seeds, crushed in a mortar
¼ tsp black peppercorns, cracked
1 cup carrots, diced
½ cup sour cream
1 Tbsp fresh parsley, chopped

✦ Cook the sausage in a heavy pot over a low flame until golden brown, breaking it into pieces the size of peas as it cooks. Remove the meat with a slotted spoon and reserve. Cook the onion, celery, garlic, and savory in the fat until softened. Add the potatoes and apples and cook for 5 minutes, stirring occasionally. Pour in the beer and chicken stock. Bring to a boil, reduce the heat, and simmer for 30 minutes. Skim the fat from the surface as the soup cooks.

Puree the soup in a blender or pass it through the fine disc of a food mill. Return to the pot, add the reserved sausage and the carrots, caraway seed, and pepper, and simmer again for 20 minutes. Adjust the consistency as necessary, by adding water to thin or by reducing over medium heat to thicken, and season to taste. Remove from the heat and stir in the sour cream. Ladle into bowls and sprinkle with the freshly chopped parsley.

Split-Pea Soup with Smoked Meat
Yield 8–10 meal-size servings

There's no trick to making a silky smooth soup of dried legumes and diced vegetables. A good split-pea soup calls for a 2-step cooking process. The peas are first simmered with the seasonings and ham bone or carcass of a smoked fowl. The meat is then removed and picked from the bones; the soup is pureed in a blender. Finally, the meat and puree are returned to the pot with the diced root vegetables, and the soup is enlivened with a fillip of seedy mustard. This is a complete meal, satisfying and nutritious on a cold day. Common crackers, hot rolls, or crusty dark bread round out the board.

4 Tbsp butter
2 cloves garlic, sliced
2 cups onions, small dice
1 tsp dried savory
1 tsp dried marjoram
½ tsp dried leaf thyme
1 bay leaf
¼ tsp crushed red pepper
A meaty ham bone or the carcass from a smoked turkey, goose, or duckling
1 lb split peas (2 cups)
10 cups cold water
1 cup carrots, ¼-inch dice
1 cup potato, ¼-inch dice
2 tsp whole-grain mustard

✦ Melt the butter, over low heat, in a large pot. Add the garlic, onions, herbs, and crushed red pepper. Cook until the onion is transparent, stirring occasionally. Add the bone or carcass, water, and the split peas. Bring to a boil and then reduce the heat so that the soup simmers gently. The liquid in the pot must be kept moving so that the peas will not stick to the bottom, but a rolling boil must be avoided. Simmer uncovered for 2 hours.

Remove the bone from the soup and allow to cool. Pick off the meat, shred into bite-size pieces, and reserve. Discard the bay leaf and puree the soup in a blender. Return the soup and meat to a clean pot. Add the potatoes and carrots and cook until these vegetables have softened, about 15 minutes. Stir in the mustard and season with salt and pepper if necessary. Usually the ham provides sufficient salt to season the soup.

When reheating leftover split-pea soup, add a little water to compensate for the thickening that takes place as the soup is stored.

Dilled Cauliflower and Carrot Soup
Yield 8–10 meal-size servings

In early autumn the flavors of these vegetables are at peak. The sweetness of carrots and the slightly sour tang of cauliflower complement each other nicely.

¼ lb unsalted butter
1 medium onion, sliced
2 lb carrots, peeled and sliced
Grating (pinch) fresh nutmeg
Pinch cayenne pepper
2 qt chicken stock, canned chicken broth, or 8 bouillon cubes in 2 qt water
1 medium head cauliflower, cored and chopped
Handful fresh dill leaves, chopped fine
Salt and pepper to taste
Fresh dill fronds for garnish

✦ Melt the butter, over low heat, in a large pot. Add the onions, carrots, and spices. Cover and stew slowly until the carrots have softened, about 20 minutes. Add the chicken stock and bring to a boil. Add the chopped cauliflower and cook until it has just softened. Cauliflower should never be overcooked. It becomes unpleasantly sour and gives off a disagreeable odor.

Puree the soup in a blender, return to a clean pot, and reheat. Add the fresh dill and adjust the consistency with more chicken stock if necessary. Season to taste and serve garnished with a frond of fresh dill.

Baked Onion Soup with Melted Cheddar and Bacon
Yield 6 servings

A simple one-dish family meal that could become a Saturday night tradition. Accompany with a crisp green salad.

6 strips bacon
3 cups onions, sliced and well packed
1 Tbsp granulated sugar
4 cloves garlic, minced
1 tsp dried sage
2 Tbsp all-purpose flour
2 Tbsp cider vinegar
One 12-oz bottle beer or ale
2 qt brown stock, canned beef broth, or 8 beef bouillon cubes in 2 qt water
2 Tbsp whole-grain mustard
6 slices stale bread
3 cups Cheddar cheese, grated
Crisp bacon strips for garnish

✦ Cook the bacon over low heat in a heavy pot. Do not use an iron pot, which will react with the acid in the onion, giving an off flavor. Remove with a slotted spoon and reserve. Increase the heat to high, add the onions to the hot bacon fat, and cook until transparent, stirring occasionally. Sprinkle in the sugar and cook until the onions are nicely browned, stirring occasionally. Lower the heat, add the garlic and sage, and cook for 1 minute. Add the flour and stir to a paste. Add the vinegar to scald, then pour in the beer and brown stock. Bring the soup to a boil, reduce to a simmer, and cook for 20 minutes. Skim the fat from the surface with a ladle. Season to taste with salt and pepper.

Ladle the hot soup into individual oven-proof soup crocks. Trim the bread so that one piece fits inside each crock, and spread each piece with a teaspoon of the mustard. Cover each crock with a bread slice, mustard side up, and place the crocks on a sheet pan. Mound each one with the grated cheese and place under a broiler, 4–6 inches from the flame. Broil until the cheese is bubbly.

Preheat oven to 500°F.

The soup can also be baked for 15 minutes in a preheated 500° F oven until the same effect is achieved. Garnish each serving with a strip of crisp bacon and serve immediately.

Freshwater Fish

✦

Sauté of Salmon with Peas and Thyme Cream

Salmon Fillets with Apple Butter

Poached Fillet of Salmon with Spring Greens

Fried Smelt or Yellow Perch with Horseradish Sauce

Walleye Pike Baked with Garlic Mayonnaise

Poached Brook Trout with Asparagus Stew

Brook Trout Stuffed with Salmon Mousse and

Tarragon Butter Sauce

Cured Lake Trout or Salmon

Hot-Smoked Freshwater Fish

Vermont's boundaries are defined by water. The Connecticut River divides it from New Hampshire, flowing from Canadian headwaters all the way to Long Island Sound. Vermont's western limits are marked by Lake Champlain, across which are seen the wooded hills of New York State. Between these natural borders, tributary streams rush down mountainsides, filling valleys with rivers and forming lakes in glacial basins.

This network of waterways yields boundless opportunities for sportsmen and sportswomen. Vermont's fish are classed as warm-water and cold-water species. Warm-water species include yellow perch, walleye, northern brown bullhead or bullpout, northern pike, chain pickerel, and largemouth and smallmouth bass. Cold-water varieties include brook, rainbow, brown, and lake trout; landlocked salmon; and smelt. The Fish and Game Department is currently reintroducing Atlantic salmon and American shad to the waters of the Connecticut River, a program which promises exciting possibilities for future fishing.

Because of Vermont's variety of native fishes and lack of a seacoast, I have restricted recipes to those made from its freshwater fishes. Seafood may be substituted for some recipes. Atlantic salmon can be used in place of landlocked salmon, fillets of white-fleshed fish such as haddock for walleye. The characteristic difference between saltwater and freshwater fish is chiefly flavor—saltwater fish generally have a blander taste as opposed to the gamey quality of freshwater species. All fish should be eaten as soon as possible after catching or purchase.

For more information on fishing in Vermont, contact Vermont Fish and Game Department, Montpelier, Vermont 05602.

Terminology

Pan-dressed—A fish prepared for pan-frying by removing the head and fins, gutting, and scaling.

Whole-dressed—A fish prepared for baking, poaching, grilling, or the barbecue. The fish is gutted and scaled, head removed but fins and tail left intact.

Steaked—A fish is gutted and scaled but not boned. Large, round fish such as salmon can be cut crosswise into steaks 1–2 inches thick. Steaks are often grilled, barbecued, poached, or baked.

Fillet—The flesh removed lengthwise from the ribcage of a fish. It may be skinless or retain the skin. The needlelike bones that remain in the fillet are usually removed with a pair of needlenose pliers before cooking.

Floating Ribs—These needlelike bones are not directly attached to the skeletal system. They extend two thirds the length of many fish, buried in the flesh. Floating ribs should be removed before preparing most recipes. They are usually visible; if not, find them by touch, running your fingertips down the internal side of the fillet. Grasp them firmly with a pair of needlenose pliers and extract as if they were splinters.

Boning Procedure—The skeletal structure of many fish is like a two-sided comb which separates the two fillets. Using a very sharp knife, lay the fish on the counter and hold it on its back. Cut through the ribs along one side of the backbone, but do not cut all the way through. Open the fish like a book. Lay the side of your knife underneath the bones, and pressing against them with the blade, cut along and behind them, sliding the knife through. Remove the bones in one piece. Repeat for the other side, removing the backbone with the ribs. On trout, the small hairlike bones protruding from the side can be pulled out with your fingers. On larger fish, such as salmon and lake trout, remove these floating ribs with a pair of needlenose pliers.

Sauté of Salmon with Peas and Thyme Cream
Yield 6 servings

The traditional Fourth of July feast includes the best the season offers: salmon, fresh garden peas, boiled new potatoes, a green salad, and a chilled Sauvignon Blanc or a Muscadet.

The Sauce

1 cup white wine
2 Tbsp shallots, chopped fine
2 cups heavy cream
2 tsp fresh thyme leaves, chopped fine
Salt and pepper to taste
Juice 1 lemon
2 cups peas, freshly shucked
Chopped fresh parsley for garnish   *(Continued)*

The Salmon

2 lb salmon fillet, skin removed; landlocked or Atlantic salmon may be used

Flour as needed for dredging

Salt and pepper

¼ cup vegetable oil

4 Tbsp butter

The Sauce

✦ Bring a pot of water to a boil, add the peas, and boil for 30 seconds. Drain immediately into a colander. Refresh the peas under cold running water and reserve.

Place the shallots and white wine in a saucepan. Reduce, over a medium flame, until there is just a trace of liquid left, about 5 minutes. Add the cream and thyme. Reduce by one-half, about 5 minutes. Season to taste with salt and pepper. Add the lemon juice, remove from the heat, and reserve.

The Salmon

✦ Using a pair of needlenose pliers or tweezers, remove the floating ribs from the salmon. You can feel the bones by running your fingers along the center of the fillet. Pull them out as if they were splinters (see Introduction to this chapter). Turn the fillet so that the skinned side is up. Slice the salmon on the bias, following the lines of connective tissue that also run on the bias. By following these lines, the fish will hold together when it is cooked. Pound the slices gently between sheets of waxed paper to produce even, well-shaped pieces about ¼ inch thick.

Salt and pepper the slices and dredge them in flour. Pat them between your hands to remove the excess flour. Heat the oil and butter in a skillet over medium-high heat. Cook the salmon in batches without overcrowding the skillet, and cook no more than a half minute to the side, being careful not to let it dry out. Keep the cooked slices warm on a platter.

Assemble the dish by warming the cooked peas in the cream sauce, adjusting the consistency as necessary by thinning with heavy cream or thickening by reduction. Spoon the creamed peas onto each plate. Top with 2–3 slices of salmon and garnish with chopped fresh parsley. Serve at once.

Salmon Fillets with Apple Butter
Yield 4 servings

The sweetness of apple butter and the sharpness of onions strike a balance between acidity and richness. They complement the gamey quality of salmon in this unusual and savory dish. Enhance the subtle sweetness by serving with corn oysters (see Chapter 6, Vegetables: Corn Oysters and Fritters), a crisp green vegetable, and a smooth California Chardonnay.

> **4 salmon fillets, 6–8 oz each; landlocked or Atlantic salmon may be used**
> **4 Tbsp butter**
> **4 cups onions, sliced thin**
> **8–12 Tbsp apple butter**

✦ Using a pair of needlenose pliers or tweezers, remove the floating ribs from the salmon fillets. You will find these bones by running your fingers along the side of the fish and pulling them out as if they were splinters (see the Introduction to this chapter). Remove the skin.

Preheat oven to 375°F.

Melt the butter over low heat in an ovenproof skillet; an iron skillet works well for this purpose. Over low heat stew the onions until they have cooked without coloring. Salt and pepper the onions to taste. Place the fillets on the bed of onions. Spread each with 2–3 tablespoons of apple butter.

Bake, on the center shelf of a preheated 375°F oven, 20–25 minutes, or until the salmon will flake easily when tested with the tines of a fork. Serve immediately, placing a fillet of salmon onto each plate nested on its bed of onions.

Poached Fillet of Salmon with Spring Greens
Yield 6 servings

New spring greens arrive as the fishing season opens. Their acid nature enhances a fish's flavor in the same way that lemon juice does. The creamy sauce and slightly crunchy vegetables complement the sweet flesh of the salmon. Serve with boiled potatoes and a slightly chilled Sancere or a Muscadet.

6 salmon fillets, 6–8 oz each; landlocked or Atlantic salmon may be used.

The Court Bouillon

2 qt cold water
1 cup white vinegar
1 medium onion, peeled and sliced
1 stalk celery, sliced
Small handful fresh parsley
2 bay leaves
½ tsp black peppercorns

The Greens

1 cup white wine or cider
2 packed cups dandelion greens
1 large handful young sorrel leaves
½ lb spinach
4 scallions, peeled and sliced thin, including the greens
1 cup heavy cream
3 oz cream cheese
Grating (pinch) fresh nutmeg
Pinch cayenne pepper
Juice 1 lemon
2 Tbsp fresh chives, chopped

The Court Bouillon

✦ Combine all ingredients in a large low-sided pot. Simmer for 30 minutes, strain through a wire strainer, and return to the pot. This broth should be kept at a simmer and not allowed to boil.

The Greens

✦ Clean all the greens and remove any tough stems. The greens should be cooked separately because they have slightly different cooking times. If necessary, improvise a steamer by placing a colander over a pot of boiling water and covering it with a lid. Otherwise, you may simply drop the greens into boiling water and cook until done.

Prepare the greens while the court bouillon is simmering. Dandelion greens take the most time. Make sure they are well washed of grit. Bring a pot of water to a boil and drop in the greens, cook about 10 minutes, and check for doneness. Drain in a colander, refresh under cold running water, and press out the excess moisture with the back of a spoon. The sorrel and spinach require little time to cook; less than half a minute will suffice. Drain them and press out the excess moisture.

Put the wine and scallions in a saucepan and reduce by one half. Add the cream, cream cheese, nutmeg, and cayenne, and reduce until thickened. Add the greens and lemon juice; stir to combine. Season to taste with salt and pepper.

The Salmon

✦ Remove the floating ribs from the salmon using a pair of needlenose pliers or a pair of tweezers. You will find these bones by running your fingers along the sides of the fish. Remove them as if they were splinters. Leave the skin on the fish; it will be much easier to remove after poaching. Refrigerate the fish until ready to cook.

Lower the salmon into the simmering court bouillon. Cook for 10 minutes to the inch, measuring the thickness of the fillet. The average fillet requires about 8 minutes. Begin counting from the moment the fish is placed in the broth. When done, remove it with a perforated spatula to a towel. Blot the excess moisture and peel away the skin.

To serve, spoon the greens onto the center of warmed plates. Spread them around so they cover most of the plate's surface. Top with a fillet of salmon, sprinkle with chives, and serve at once.

Fried Smelt or Yellow Perch with Horseradish Sauce
Yield 4 servings

Smelt are jigged through thick ice during the long winter ice-fishing season. Their diminutive size does not preclude their popularity among sport fishermen. The best for frying are 6 inches long. These smaller fish are easier to handle and crisp up more quickly. Since the bones have not yet hardened, these fish can be eaten whole. This recipe is also good for small yellow perch, which take a little longer to cook; their bones cannot be eaten.

Serve the fish piled on a platter or in a basket lined with a cloth napkin, together with lemon wedges and cruets of vinegar along with the horseradish dipping sauce. Accompany with baked potatoes and a large tossed salad. Mugs of beer, a white table wine, iced tea with lemon, or sparkling cider are perfect accompaniments for this very informal fun feast.

The Sauce

> ½ cup fresh horseradish, grated
> Juice 1 lemon
> 1 small onion, grated
> ½ cup sour cream
> 2 Tbsp fresh parsley, chopped
> 1 cup heavy cream
> Salt and freshly ground pepper to taste

The Smelt or Yellow Perch

> 8–12 smelt per person, dressed, leaving heads and tails; or 4–6 perch, which must be scaled as well
> Flour as needed to coat the fish
> 3 eggs, beaten
> 1 cup all-purpose flour
> 1 cup stone-ground cornmeal

The Sauce

✦ Peel the horseradish root, wash, and dry. Using the fine side of a hand grater or the fine disc of a food processor, grate as much horseradish as you like. The sauce will be very spicy when first made but will lose its kick as it sits. It will not keep overnight so make only as much as you will use.

Toss the grated horseradish with the lemon juice, and combine the onion, sour cream, parsley, and horseradish in a bowl. In a separate bowl whip the cream to soft peaks and fold this into the sour cream mixture. Season to taste with salt and pepper. Refrigerate until service.

The Smelt or Yellow Perch

✦ Wash the smelt and dry them with a towel; be sure to scale the perch as well. Arrange 3 pans for breading the fish: flour in the first, beaten egg in the second, and flour and cornmeal mixed together in the third. Roll the fish in the flour, patting to remove any excess; dip in the egg; and, finally, roll in the cornmeal mixture. Use one hand for the dry mixture and the other for the egg. This will prevent you from continually coating your fingers as you work.

Heat 2 inches of shortening or lard in a heavy pot over medium heat. Try to maintain a temperature around 375°F. Fry the smelt in small batches, 2–2½ minutes per batch, or perch, 3–3½ minutes per batch. Drain them on absorbent paper and keep the first batches warm in a low oven while cooking the remaining fish.

Walleye Pike Baked with Garlic Mayonnaise
Yield 4 servings

Although commonly called a pike, the walleye is actually a member of the perch family. An important sport fish, it has fine, sweet flesh that lends itself to almost any preparation. Serve this dish with grilled tomatoes, a crisp green vegetable, crusty bread, and a slightly chilled Fume Blanc or Graves wine.

2 lb walleye, filleted and skin removed
1 recipe homemade mayonnaise (see Chapter 7, Preserves and Condiments: Mayonnaise)
1 whole head garlic, squeezed through a garlic press or minced
3 Tbsp fresh parsley, chopped
White wine as needed

(Continued)

✦ *Preheat oven to 450°F.*

A full recipe of homemade mayonnaise, which yields 2 cups, is more than you will need for this quantity of fish. If you are a garlic lover, use of the remaining mayonnaise should not present much of a problem. Make the mayonnaise using olive oil, if you wish, and finish it with lemon juice instead of vinegar. Add the chopped parsley and garlic. It will be better if you pass the garlic through a press as this process intensifies its flavor.

Generously butter a baking dish and lay in the fillets, skinned side down, without touching. Cover the walleye with a quarter-inch layer of mayonnaise, and add the wine so that it barely covers the bottom of the pan. Place the dish in a preheated 450° F oven and bake 20–22 minutes. The fish is done when it is opaque and will flake easily if tested with the tines of a fork. The mayonnaise will be puffed and golden brown. Remove the walleye with a perforated spatula directly onto dinner plates. Serve immediately.

Poached Brook Trout with Asparagus Stew
Yield 4 servings

The natural protective coating on a trout reacts to the acidity of the court bouillon and turns the fish a surprising chalky blue. Serve with broiled tomatoes, crusty bread, and a fine white Burgundy or a graceful Chardonnay.

4 fresh trout about 12 oz each, dressed weight, boned after cooking (see the Introduction to this chapter)

The Asparagus Stew
2 lb fresh asparagus, trimmed and peeled
2 shallots, peeled and chopped fine
½ cup white wine
2 Tbsp white vinegar
½ cup heavy cream
6 Tbsp unsalted butter, cut into pats
Salt and pepper to taste
1 Tbsp chopped fresh chives for garnish

The Court Bouillon

2 qt cold water
1 cup white vinegar
1 Tbsp salt
1 medium onion, sliced
1 stalk celery, sliced
Small handful fresh parsley
2 bay leaves
½ tsp black peppercorns

The Court Bouillon

✦ Combine all of the ingredients in a pot and simmer for 30 minutes. Strain through a wire sieve. Return to the pot and reserve.

The Asparagus Stew

✦ Drop the asparagus into boiling water and cook, uncovered, until the asparagus is crisp-tender, about 2 minutes. Plunge immediately into ice water and allow it to cool completely. Slice the asparagus on the bias into ½-inch pieces. Pat dry with a towel and reserve.

Make the sauce for the asparagus before you cook the trout. Add the asparagus when you remove the trout from the court bouillon.

Place the shallots, white wine, and vinegar in a saucepan over medium heat, and reduce until there is just a trace of liquid left. Add the heavy cream and reduce by one half. Increase the heat to high. Add the asparagus and butter to the pan. Swirl the pan to combine the ingredients. Cook until the asparagus is just heated through, just 1–2 minutes. The sauce should be thick enough to coat the back of a spoon. Season to taste with salt and pepper. Keep warm until ready to serve.

The Trout

✦ The trout should be as fresh as possible for this dish, preferably just caught. Have the court bouillon at a rolling boil and plunge the trout into it. When the bouillon returns to a boil, reduce the heat, cover, and cook very slowly for 5 minutes. The trout will be curled, chalky blue, and ever so delicate to handle. Remove the trout using two perforated spatulas or slotted spoons onto a towel. Let rest for 1 minute to drain the excess moisture. *(Continued)*

The bones are easily removed from the cooked trout in one piece. This can be accomplished with the fish still intact after the surgery. The skeletal structure is like a two-sided comb, which separates the halves of the fish. Run a butter knife or the back of a spoon between the top fillet and the bones. Open the trout like a book and lift out the skeleton in one piece (see Introduction to this chapter). Place the fillets back into their original position.

Place the trout onto individual serving plates. Spoon the asparagus stew over it and sprinkle with the chives. Serve immediately.

Brook Trout Stuffed with Salmon Mousse and Tarragon Butter Sauce
Yield 6 servings

Fresh brook trout filled with airy, coral-colored salmon mousse makes a dramatic presentation. It is rich, yet light enough to be included in a dinner of several courses. Serve with asparagus, snow peas, or fiddle-heads; boiled new potatoes; and a tossed salad of watercress and butter lettuce. A crisp white wine such as Chablis or a Bordeaux goes well with the elegant trout.

The Trout and Salmon Mousse

6 trout, 8–10 oz each, boned (see the Introduction to this chapter)
12 oz scrap pieces of salmon, skinned and boned
1 Tbsp tomato paste
1 egg white
1 Tbsp lemon juice
1 Tbsp brandy or sherry
⅛ tsp freshly grated nutmeg
Pinch cayenne pepper
¾ tsp salt
¾ cup heavy cream
1 Tbsp fresh parsley, chopped
Parchment paper to cover fish
Butter to cover 1 side of parchment paper

3 Tbsp shallots, chopped fine
1 cup white wine
Lemon wedge for garnish with cold trout

The Sauce

The cooking liquid from the trout
1 Tbsp fresh tarragon, chopped
½ tsp black peppercorns, cracked in a mortar
½ cup heavy cream
¼ lb unsalted butter, cut into pats
Salt to taste
1–2 Tbsp water, if necessary, to emulsify sauce
Fresh parsley, chopped, for garnish

The Trout and Salmon Mousse

✦ Cut the salmon into 1-inch cubes and puree in a food processor. Add the tomato paste, egg white, brandy, lemon juice, spices, and salt. Run the machine until the mixture is smooth. Add the heavy cream, running the machine until the cream is just incorporated. Turn this puree into a bowl, stir in the chopped parsley, and cover with plastic wrap. Refrigerate at least 1 hour before stuffing the trout.

Trout may be purchased already boned from the fish store. Boning your own trout is not difficult; the only tool you need is a small, very sharp knife. Begin by dressing the trout and cutting off the head. The boning will be done from the inside rather than through the skin side. Lay the fish on the counter and hold it on its back. Cut through the ribs along one side of the backbone but do not cut all the way through. Open the trout like a book. Lay the side of your knife underneath the bones and, pressing against them with the blade, cut along and behind them, sliding the knife through. Remove the bones in one piece. Repeat for the other side, removing the backbone with the ribs. The few hairlike bones protruding from the side of the thick end can be pulled out with your fingers. (See the illustration at the beginning of this chapter.)

Preheat oven to 400°F.

Pat the trout dry with a towel and season with salt and pepper. Divide the salmon mousse stuffing equally among the trout. Generously butter a stainless steel, flame-proof baking pan, and sprinkle it with the chopped shallots. Lay the fish in a single layer, without touching, and pour in the wine.

Slather one side of a piece of parchment paper with butter. Place the paper, butter side down, on top of the fish. Heat the pan over a burner until it just comes to a boil. Place the pan in a preheated 400°F oven and bake for 15 minutes. Remove the pan from the oven and carefully drain the cooking liquid into a saucepan. Keep the trout covered in a warm place while making the sauce.

The Sauce

✦ Reduce the cooking liquid over a medium-high flame with the tarragon and pepper until syrupy. Add the heavy cream and reduce until quite thick, 3–5 minutes. Reduce the heat to low and gradually add the butter, swirling it into the sauce. The sauce should be white in color and thick enough to coat the back of a spoon. If the sauce "breaks," add a tablespoon or two of water to emulsify it. Season to taste with salt. Pour into a warmed sauceboat and pass at the table.

Remove the fish to a cutting board with the aid of a long, perforated spatula. Cut off the heads and fins. Peel away the skin with the aid of a small knife. Lay the fish side by side on a serving platter. Spoon a teaspoon of the sauce over each trout and decorate with sprigs of parsley or spray of fresh tarragon. Serve immediately.

A Variation

✦ This dish may also be served on a cold buffet. After cooking, remove them to a platter, cover, and refrigerate overnight. Remove the skin, fins, heads, and tails. Cut the trout into 1-inch slices and arrange on a platter to show off the white trout encircling the beautiful pink salmon mousse.

Cured Lake Trout or Salmon
Yield 1 fillet (about 2 pounds)

Curing is a simple process that "cooks" the fish by breaking down the proteins with salt instead of with heat. The results are very impressive for the small amount of work involved. Elegant on a buffet or as a first course, serve the thin sliced fish with dark bread, wedges of lemon, freshly grated horseradish, and champagne.

A large lake trout or salmon (about 5 lb)
For each fillet (twice this amount will be needed for the entire fish)
    2 Tbsp rum, applejack, or brandy
    About ½ cup maple syrup, or as needed
    1 Tbsp black peppercorns, cracked
    ¼ cup kosher salt
    ½–1 cup fresh dill, chopped fine
    Good handful of spruce boughs—use the branch tips having fresh
      green needles

✦ Dress and fillet the fish, discarding the head and tail. Save the carcass and trimmings to make salmon bisque (see Chapter 2, Stocks and Soups: Bisque of Salmon with Peas). Using a pair of needlenose pliers or tweezers, remove the floating ribs from the fish. You will find these bones by running your fingers along the side of the fillet. Pull them out as if they were splinters (see the Introduction to this chapter). Leave the skin on the fish; this will make it easier to handle and slice.

On a large sheet of aluminum foil, lay down a bed of spruce boughs. Place the fish skin side down on the branches. Sprinkle with the liquor and generously brush with maple syrup. Sprinkle the cracked peppercorns over the fish. Add an even layer of salt over the flesh and, finally, cover with the dill. Wrap the fish tightly in the foil and place in a shallow pan, skin side down. Put a board or flat pan on top of this package. Place a 2-pound weight on top (2 cans of soup, for example). This will compress the flesh of the fish, making it easier to slice.

Refrigerate for 3 days. Unwrap and discard the pine boughs. Using a long, thin knife, slice the cured fish on the bias as thin as possible. Turn the blade as it touches the skin so that you do not slice through the skin. A cured lake trout will have a beautiful translucence that is slightly golden in color. Salmon turns out a glowing rose or coral tint. The flavor is so delicate that you may wish to serve this accompanied merely with cruets of red wine vinegar, cold pressed olive oil, and buttered crusty bread.

Hot-Smoked Freshwater Fish

Before refrigeration, smoking was used to preserve food. Today we continue the practice but use it to enhance flavor. Refrigeration makes hot-smoking possible and thus reduces the required smoking time from weeks to hours. The following excerpt from the 1808 edition of Lucy Emerson's *New England Cookery* illustrates the change:

To Make the Best Bacon

To each ham put one ounce saltpetre, one pint bay salt, one pint molasses, shake together six or eight weeks, or when a large quantity is together, bast them with the liquor everyday; when taken out to dry, smoak three weeks with cobs or malt fumes. To every ham may be added a cheek if you stow away in a barrel and not alter the composition, some add a shoulder. For transportation or exportation, double the period of smoaking.

Yes, that's 3 weeks in the smokehouse, 6 weeks if you were going on a trip.

Fish, cheese, sausage, duck, goose, turkey, and pork products respond well to smoking. Here is a technique for fish angled from Vermont waters. The process is less complicated than the one for meats. Any fish can be smoked, but some types produce superior results. The lake trout is the best, in my opinion, followed by salmon, walleye, brook, rainbow and brown trout, smelt, eel, and bullpout. Fish with oily flesh produce firm, moist results. The method for all of the above is the same. It involves a 3-step process of brining, air drying, and smoking.

Smoked fish can be served warm, directly from the smoker, accompanied by coleslaw, corn on the cob, baked potatoes, and cold beer or iced tea with lemon—surely a memorable summer feast. The fish can also be refrigerated overnight to set the flesh. Slice and serve it with freshly grated horseradish, spicy mustard, crusty bread, sweet butter, and champagne.

Brining

2 cups pickling salt
1 cup brown sugar
1 gallon water
Handful of whole spices, herbs, or flavorings, if desired. (*Note:* Powdered spices or herbs will discolor the fish.)

✦ A note on salt: Every good supermarket has pickling salt, so labeled, made by the leading manufacturers of table salt, and this is what you should use in pre-treating meat for smoke-cooking. Table salt should not be used. Table salt often contains iodine (the container will say so), and iodine can change the color of the flesh. Even noniodized table salt is undesirable for brining as it contains "fillers"—starches and other ingredients which prevent caking in damp weather. The term "kosher" does not guarantee the right salt for brining since kosher salt comes in a number of different cuts—flaky, fluffy, etc.—whereas pickling salt is always the same cut. You should also avoid sea salt; it contains many minerals which can react in unwanted ways with meat and vegetables. At all costs, avoid "solar salt," which is likely to contain large amounts of unwanted animal and vegetable matter as well as minerals.

Bring all ingredients to a boil. Remove from heat and cool to less than room temperature. The addition of a few ice cubes will expedite the process. Do not use until completely cool.

Prepare the fish by gutting it and rinsing with cold water. Fish that are more than 2 inches thick should be filleted as well as fish weighing more than 5 pounds. It is difficult for the smoke to penetrate a thickness of more than 2 inches without first drying out the exterior. The skin and rib bones should not be removed.

Place the fish in the brine so that it is totally submerged. Small fish (under 2 pounds) require about 2 hours to leach out the blood. Larger fish require 4–6 hours and eels a full 24 hours in the brine, which should be kept below room temperature at all times. Placing the pan containing the solution on the cellar floor will keep it at a satisfactory temperature. As the blood is leached from the fish, the brine will become cloudy.

Remove the fish from the brine and rinse under cold running water. Hang or lay the fish on a wire rack in a cool place to dry. All moisture on the outside of the fish must be removed so that the fish doesn't develop a sour flavor when smoked; 4–6 hours is required to develop the requisite dry-shiny finish. Blowing an electric fan on the fish can reduce the drying time to about 2 hours and is recommended.

Smoking

✦ The smoker should be prepared and preheated before putting in the fish. It is important to maintain a constant temperature between 150° and

175°F, preferably closer to the lesser figure. Higher temperatures will produce steam and will cause the flesh to flake rather than acquire a firm texture. Small fish may require as little as 2 hours and larger ones up to 6 hours. Average fish such as 1- to 1½-pound trout take 3 hours. A filleted side of salmon or lake trout will take 4 hours. With practice you will be able to discern doneness by the color and firm feel of the flesh.

Use only nonresinous hardwoods such as maple, any fruitwood, beech, or oak as your fuel. A mixture of dry and green woods will keep the coals smoldering slowly and steadily. A slow-burning, smoky fire is needed. Heat-producing flames should be extinguished. Experiment with a variety of hardwoods, with corncobs, branches of fresh herbs, or other flavorings added to scent the smoke.

There are a variety of commercial smokers on the market; a model available through L. L. Bean is very popular. You can also construct one yourself from a barrel or an old refrigerator (this should be childproofed for safety). Whatever type you purchase or build, a smoker needs to have an externally mounted thermometer. It is as essential to regulate the heat generated by a smoker as by an oven.

White Meats and Poultry

✦

Roast Loin of Pork with Maple Mustard Sauce

Tenderloin of Pork with Mushrooms and Horseradish

Veal Stew with Parsley Dumplings

Escallops of Veal with Chanterelles

Veal and Morel Sausages

Stuffed Escallops of Turkey

Maple-Glazed Turkey with Cornbread Stuffing
and Cider Sauce

Pheasant Roasted with Cepes

Herbed Chicken Cutlets

Summer Succotash with Chicken

Pot-Roasted Chicken with Cracklings

Rabbit Pâté

White meats come from a variety of animals; they are grouped together arbitrarily, solely because of the color. Their common characteristic is a comparatively lower percentage of fat by weight than red meats. Even pork, through selective breeding and diet, has entered this lower fat category. The fat content of modern porkers has been reduced from an average of 15 percent down to a mere 5 percent.

Domesticated white meats need to be cooked completely through. Although this temperature varies with the animal, the roasting temperatures I have given in recipes represent the lowest level of the temperature range. When checking the internal temperature of veal, pork, turkey, and chicken, insert the thermometer into the thickest part of the meat; on fowl this is the thigh joint. Leave the thermometer in the meat 20–30 seconds to obtain an accurate reading. To determine the doneness of the meat, bear in mind that a roast needs to rest for 15–30 minutes after it has been removed from the oven. The larger the roast, the longer the rest: a chicken requires the shorter period, a Thanksgiving turkey 30–40 minutes. During this resting period the internal temperature will climb an additional 10–15 degrees. The rest allows the juices, driven to the center of the roast by thermal convection, to redistribute throughout the meat. This resting also permits the tensed muscle fibers to relax, producing a more tender result.

Carving Poultry

To carve a chicken or turkey, have a warmed platter at hand for the sliced meat. After the bird has rested, place it breast-side up on a carving board. Use a long, thin, sharp knife and a fork to hold the bird still while carving.

Begin by severing the joint between the drumstick and thigh. Remove the drumstick and slice it if preferred. Arrange the pieces attractively on the platter. Next, slice the thigh flesh until the hip socket is exposed. Cut through the joint, twisting the knife slightly, but do not pry, which can break the tip of the knife. Cut through the wing joint and divide in two if large. Remove the wishbone at the neck opening, and make an incision lengthwise along the breast bone. Slice the breast meat thin, across the grain, starting at the neck and working the length of the bird. Carve only as much as you think will be eaten. The meat will retain its moisture better if left intact on the carcass.

Roast Loin of Pork with Maple Mustard Sauce
Yield 6–8 servings

These days pork has considerably less fat content than it did when I was growing up, but it still is juicy if it is not overcooked. This fine roast emerges from the oven shiny and crisp with that special aroma that only pork has. Accompany the roast with mashed potatoes, glazed carrots, a green vegetable, and cranberry apple conserve, or baked apples. Serve with a German-style white wine, cider, or a fruit wine such as pear.

The Pork
4 ½–5 lb rib or loin end pork roast
1 Tbsp rubbed (ground) sage
1 Tbsp leaf thyme
1 Tbsp rosemary, crumbled
1 tsp allspice, ground
1 tsp black pepper, ground

The Sauce
3 Tbsp butter
1 medium onion, chopped fine
1 tsp leaf thyme
1 tsp rubbed (ground) sage
Pinch allspice
3 Tbsp all-purpose flour
2 Tbsp cider vinegar
1 cup sweet cider
2 cups chicken stock, canned chicken broth, or 2 bouillon cubes in
    2 cups water
¼ cup maple syrup
1 Tbsp whole-grain prepared mustard

The Pork
✦ A full pork loin has two parts, the rib end and the loin end; both ends are suitable for roasting. The rib end has more fat marbling in the meat and is easier to slice. The loin end includes the tenderloin, which must be carved separately. *(Continued)*

If you purchase the rib end, remove the blade bone at the large end of the roast. Cut underneath the layer of fat, lay the blade of your knife on the flat bone, and cut around it. This ensures even cooking. Otherwise, the smaller end dries out before the large end is done. Tie the fat cap over the roast so that the meat doesn't shrink away during cooking.

The loin end requires no preparation other than paring down the fat cap very thin. Mix the herbs and spices together and rub them all over the meat. Put the roast, on a roasting rack set in a shallow pan to catch the drippings, on the center shelf of a preheated 450°F oven. Reduce the heat to 325° and roast 2¼–2½ hours. The roast is done when an instant-read thermometer registers 160° when it is inserted in the thickest part of the meat. The roast should rest for at least 20 minutes before carving.

The Sauce

✦ Prepare the sauce while the roast is in the oven. Melt the butter in a saucepan over low heat. Cook the onion, herbs, and allspice until the onion has softened. Sprinkle in the flour and stir to a paste; cook until it loses its shine, about 3 minutes. Add the vinegar and stir until smooth. Pour in the stock, cider, and maple syrup and stir again until smooth. Simmer the sauce until thickened to your liking. Add the mustard and season to taste with salt and pepper. Pour into a warmed sauceboat and pass at the table.

Serving the Roast

✦ Remove the strings from the roast. Lay the blade of a sharp knife flat against the bones and cut along them. Remove the meat in one piece. Slice the roast thin, arranging the pieces on a warm platter, and serve at once.

Tenderloin of Pork with Mushrooms and Horseradish
Yield 4 servings

Pork tenderloins are choice, versatile, and tender. They can be barbecued, sautéed, roasted, baked in parchment, or stir-fried. This roasted and sliced tenderloin is napped with a sauce in which sweet cider, sour cream, and mushrooms are sparked by fresh horseradish. Serve this creamy dish with cabbage pancakes, peas, carrots, and a fruity German-style white wine or sparkling cider.

Two 1-lb pork tenderloins, trimmed
Flour as needed to dredge the pork
1 Tbsp butter
1 Tbsp vegetable oil
1 small onion, chopped fine
½ lb mushrooms, quartered
1 cup sweet cider
½ cup sour cream
2 Tbsp fresh horseradish, grated fine
2 Tbsp fresh dill, chopped, for garnish

✦ *Preheat oven to 425°F.*

Pat the tenderloins dry with a cloth and season them with salt and pepper. Dredge them with flour and pat them between your hands to remove the excess. Melt the butter and vegetable oil over medium-high heat in a heavy skillet with an ovenproof handle.

Brown the tenderloin on all sides and remove it to a plate. Reduce the heat and add the mushrooms and onions. Cook until the vegetables have softened, stirring occasionally. Pour in the cider and scrape up any browned bits clinging to the pan. Return the pork to the pan and place in a preheated 425°F oven. Cook until the pork feels firm to the touch and is cooked through, 20–25 minutes. Remove the pork to a platter and keep warm. The pork should be allowed to rest for 10 minutes before slicing.

Place the pan over medium-high heat and reduce the sauce by two-thirds. Remove the pan from the heat and stir in the sour cream and horseradish. Return to the burner and reheat without boiling; season to taste.

Slice on the bias into ½-inch pieces. Arrange the slices on a serving platter. Spoon the sauce over the pork and sprinkle with freshly chopped dill.

Veal Stew with Parsley Dumplings
Yield 8 servings

After a day outdoors this one-dish meal warms the soul. Tender veal, parsnips, peas, and fluffy dumplings flecked with parsley are served up in a steaming, rich broth. Such a simple repast calls for an unassertive wine—a Beaujolais or Muscadet.

The Stew

Butter to brown veal
2 lb stewing veal, cut into 1-inch cubes
1 lb carrots, peeled and sliced
1 lb parsnips, peeled and sliced
1 medium onion, peeled and chopped fine
8 oz peas
1 Tbsp fresh parsley, chopped
2 tsp rubbed (ground) sage
1 tsp leaf thyme
1 tsp savory, ground
2 cups dry white wine
10 cups brown stock, canned beef broth, or bouillon

The Dumplings

1 cup unbleached all-purpose flour
½ tsp salt
2 tsp baking powder
Good grating nutmeg
1 egg, beaten
2 Tbsp melted butter
⅓ cup milk
4 Tbsp chopped fresh parsley

The Stew

◆ Melt some butter in a heavy pot set on medium-high heat. Brown the veal in batches, adding more butter as needed. Remove the meat to a bowl and reserve. Lower the heat and cook the onions and herbs until the onion has softened. Add the white wine and reduce by one-half, about

8–10 minutes over medium heat. Return the veal to the pot; pour in the brown stock. Simmer uncovered for 1¼ hours.

When the veal is tender, add the carrots and cook for 15 more minutes. Then add the parsnips. When the stew returns to a simmer (do not allow it to boil), add the dumplings. Cover and steam for 15 minutes. When the dumplings are done, add the peas, which require no more than a half-minute to cook.

The Dumplings

✦ Sift the flour, salt, baking powder, and nutmeg together into a mixing bowl. Stir the parsley into the flour with a fork to ensure an even distribution of ingredients. Add the remaining ingredients. Work quickly into a soft, sticky dough. Drop the dough by the tablespoonful into the simmering stew. Cover and steam for 15 minutes. Do not boil or the dumplings will fall apart. This yields about a dozen dumplings.

Place a dumpling or two in a wide, shallow bowl and ladle the stew over them. Serve at once.

Escallops of Veal with Chanterelles
Yield 4 servings

Chanterelles, one of the most prized of all edible mushrooms, are indigenous to the North Country. Characteristically funnel-shaped and firm of flesh, they have a scent reminiscent of apricots. Enriched with cream and lightly flavored with herbs, they are dished up over tender sautéed veal for a special summer meal. Serve with rice and a simply steamed or quickly sautéed vegetable. Accompany with a fruity German-style white wine.

The Chanterelle Sauce

3 Tbsp butter
1 lb small chanterelles, cleaned and trimmed
1 Tbsp onion, chopped fine
2 Tbsp tarragon vinegar
1 cup heavy cream
Salt and pepper to taste

(Continued)

The Veal

1½ lb sliced veal top round or loin
All-purpose flour as needed for dredging
Unsalted butter as needed
Vegetable oil as needed
Juice 1 lemon
2 Tbsp fresh chives, chopped for garnish

The Chanterelle Sauce

✦ Pick over the mushrooms, making sure that all dirt and pine needles have been removed. Melt the butter in a saucepan over medium heat. Add the chanterelles and onion, and cook until the chanterelles have given up their juices, about 10 minutes. Remove the chanterelles to a bowl with a slotted spoon and reserve. Add the vinegar and reduce the liquid until syrupy. Add the cream and reduce until thick enough to coat the back of a spoon. Return the mushrooms to the sauce, cook until the sauce seems thick enough, and season to taste with salt and pepper. The total time for making the sauce is about 10 minutes. Keep the sauce warm or reheat it when you are ready to spoon it over the veal.

The Veal

✦ Pound the sliced veal between 2 sheets of waxed paper to a uniform thickness of ⅛ inch. Pat the meat dry with a cloth and season lightly with salt and pepper. Flour the veal on both sides and pat with your hands to remove the excess.

Melt some butter in a large skillet, with an equal amount of vegetable oil to fortify it, over high heat. Cook the veal, a few pieces at a time, until lightly browned on both sides. It will be firm to the touch after just 2–3 minutes of cooking time. Depending upon the size of your skillet you will have to cook the veal in 2–3 batches. Replenish the cooking fat as needed. Keep the cooked veal warm.

When the veal has finished cooking, pour off the fat from the pan. Return the veal to the pan and squeeze in the lemon juice, bathing the escallops in the liquid. Arrange the veal on a warm serving platter, spoon the chanterelle sauce over it, and garnish with chopped fresh chives. Serve immediately.

Veal and Morel Sausages
Yield 30 sausages

These sausages can be served as a first course or as the main attraction. Boiled new potatoes, goat cheese, crusty bread, a variety of mustards, and a salad of bitter greens such as curly endive, watercress, or spinach would round out the meal nicely. Although lager is usually considered an appropriate beverage, these delicately flavored sausages call for a complementary wine. A flowery white Alsatian or a handsome Merlot would do admirably.

2 lb veal, in 1-inch cubes
2 lb pork butt or shoulder, in 1-inch cubes
2 lb fresh pork fat, in 1-inch cubes
2 Tbsp kosher salt
1½ oz dried morels
½ cup good Madeira or sherry
1 cup fresh white bread crumbs
½ tsp nutmeg, freshly grated
1½ tsp leaf thyme
1½ tsp tarragon
1½ tsp marjoram
2 Tbsp chopped fresh parsley
1 tsp black peppercorns, cracked
Hog casing as needed, about 20 feet
Cold water to cover sausages
2 Tbsp white vinegar to add to cooking water

✦ Put the morels in a saucepan, cover with water, and cover tightly. Bring to a boil, remove from the heat, and leave to steep for 1 hour. Drain the mushrooms, rinse them to remove any grit, and cut off and discard the tough stems. Chop the morels coarsely, put into a bowl with the Madeira and bread crumbs, stir to combine, and reserve.

While the morels are being reconstituted, trim and cut the meats into 1-inch cubes. Put the meats into a bowl and toss with the salt, herbs, and spices. The mixture should be refrigerated for 1 hour or placed in a single layer on a sheet pan and put into the freezer for 15 minutes. It is essential

(Continued)

that the meats are cold and firm before being ground; otherwise, a mushy sausage will result.

Pass the mixture through the coarse (¼-inch) disc of a meat grinder. If you are using an electric model, set it at low speed to prevent overgrinding. Never use a food processor to make sausage, for a processor shreds unevenly, eventually producing a puree rather than an evenly ground mixture. Massage the morels and bread crumbs into the ground meats. Cover the mixture and refrigerate overnight so that the flavors can ripen and develop.

Cut the casing into manageable lengths of 3–4 feet and rinse the lengths under cold running water. Then soak the casings in a bowl of cold water for a few minutes to soften. Attach the sausage nozzle onto your meat grinder. Thread one of the casings onto the nozzle and slowly work the sausage mixture into it. The meat should fill the casing. Avoid air bubbles and do not pack it too tightly.

Once the lengths of casing have been filled, twist the sausages at 4-inch intervals to form links. When making the twists, alternate them clockwise and then counterclockwise so they will not unravel. If you do not intend to cook all the links, the sausage freezes quite well for future use.

To Cook the Sausages

✦ Place the sausages in a pot and cover with cold water. Add a couple of tablespoons of white vinegar (the acidity of the vinegar will help to coagulate the proteins, thus preventing the sausages from bursting). Heat until the water barely quivers—do not let it boil. Simmer slowly for 5 minutes, drain, and refresh the sausages under cool water. You can now refrigerate them until you are ready to serve or proceed with the cooking. Cut into individual links and fry over medium-low heat in some butter until nicely browned. Serve at once.

Stuffed Escallops of Turkey
Yield 4 servings

Turkeys are native to North America. Today's domesticated bird is the product of generations of selective breeding from that wild fowl known to the first European settlers. Turkey can be served plain or dressed up in endless ways. It is lean, high in protein, economical, and full of flavor.

Accompany the escallops with rice and a crisp vegetable such as Brussels sprouts, asparagus, or fiddleheads. A fruit conserve is always a pleasant addition. Lemon wedges and tarragon vinegar provide a nice tangy contrast. Easy-going white wines—Soave, Muscadet, or a German Kabinett—complement this inexpensive and appealing dinner.

2 lb boneless turkey breast
2 Tbsp butter
½ lb mushrooms, sliced
1 lemon
2 Tbsp onion, chopped fine
½ cup white wine
2 Tbsp fresh chives, chopped
1 cup Swiss cheese, grated
2 tsp Dijon mustard
Flour as needed for dredging
2 eggs, beaten
Fine stale bread crumbs as needed
2 Tbsp butter fortified with 2 Tbsp vegetable oil to cook the escallops

✦ Hold your knife perpendicular to the grain of the meat and slice the breast into 8 equal slices. Pound the slices between 2 sheets of waxed paper so that the meat is of uniform size and thickness; each slice should measure roughly 4 x 6 inches. Refrigerate until ready to stuff.

Melt the butter over low heat. Cook the onions until softened, add the mushrooms, and squeeze over them the juice from half the lemon. Add the white wine and increase the heat to medium-high. Cook until all the moisture has evaporated. It may be necessary to lower the heat near the end so the mushrooms do not burn. Turn into a bowl and toss with the cheese, chives, and mustard. Season to taste with salt and pepper. Allow this mixture to come to room temperature before proceeding with the recipe.

(Continued)

Season the sliced turkey with salt and pepper. Lay 4 slices out on the counter and cover them with the stuffing, leaving ½ inch uncovered around the edges so they can be sealed to the remaining escallops, placed on top to form sandwiches. Flour the turkey and pat lightly to remove the excess. Dip in the beaten egg and finally in the bread crumbs. Pat the crumbs with your hands to ensure a good coating and press around the edges for a good seal. Place on waxed paper and refrigerate until ready to cook.

Melt a mixture of butter fortified with an equal amount of vegetable oil in a large skillet over medium heat. Cook the turkey until golden brown, 4–5 minutes. Turn the escallops, cook for a further 4–5 minutes, and remove to a serving platter. Pour off the cooking fat and add two tablespoons of butter to the pan and heat until the contents just start to take on color. Toss in a tablespoon of chopped fresh parsley and squeeze the juice from the remaining half lemon into the pan; this will sizzle and foam. Pour this mixture over the turkey. Serve immediately with lemon wedges and a cruet of tarragon vinegar.

Maple-Glazed Turkey with Cornbread Stuffing and Cider Sauce
Yield 20 or more servings

Vermont-grown turkeys are in demand for the holidays and for a good reason. Birds raised in a cold climate develop a layer of fat after the first frost. This layer keeps the Vermont turkey naturally moist and sweet during roasting—the natural version of the self-basting bird. When choosing your holiday turkey, pay the extra for a freshly killed bird. What a difference! If you raise your own, try to get Rosa Linda poults. They grow into adult birds quickly and have breasts so large they are concave at the breastbone.

Serve with a selection of green and root vegetables, relishes, and a cranberry conserve. Mugs of sweet or hard cider are traditional for the holiday feast. When choosing wine, remember the slightly gamey quality of turkey. White Zinfandel is a good choice although a Beaujolais served at 55°F might be even better.

20–25 lb freshly killed turkey

The Stuffing

    6 cups stale white bread, broken into ½-inch pieces
    6 cups stale cornbread (one recipe johnnycake crumbled; see Chapter
        8, Breads and Breakfast Cakes: Vermont Johnnycake)
    4 medium onions, peeled and sliced
    6 stalks celery, diced
    2 lb slab bacon, rind removed, in ¼-inch dice
    1 Tbsp each: rubbed (ground) sage, marjoram, leaf thyme, savory
    3 Tbsp fresh parsley, chopped
    ¼ tsp black pepper, freshly ground
    ½ cup bourbon whiskey (optional)
    4 eggs, beaten
    1 cup sweet cider

Roasting the Turkey

    2 carrots, peeled and halved lengthwise
    4 stalks celery, peeled
    2 medium onions, peeled and sliced
    Reserved bacon drippings
    1 cup maple syrup, dark amber

The Sauce

    The vegetables from the roasting pan
    3 cups sweet cider
    Salt and pepper to taste

The Stuffing

✦ Crumble the breads onto a sheet pan and leave overnight to get stale.
The next day place them in a large bowl. Cook the bacon over medium-
low heat until golden brown. Remove with a slotted spoon and add to the
bread. Pour off all but a quarter cup of the drippings. Reserve the extra
bacon drippings for basting the turkey.

Cook the vegetables and herbs in the remaining fat until softened.

Increase the heat to high, pour in the bourbon and flambé. When the flame subsides, add the cider and cook until reduced by one-half, about 3 minutes at high heat. Add the vegetables, eggs, and pepper to the crumbled bread, and mix with a spoon until well combined. Season the cavity of the turkey. Loosely stuff both the front and rear cavities. Truss well with cotton butcher's twine.

Roasting the Turkey

✦ The turkey will be roasted on a bed of vegetables. This will raise it above the bottom of the pan, preventing it from stewing in its own juices. The vegetables will also be the foundation for the cider sauce.

Preheat oven to 325°F.

Prepare the vegetables and lay them in a commodious roasting pan, alternating the carrots and celery across the pan. Scatter the onions over the carrots and celery. Place the turkey on the vegetables and brush it all over with some of the reserved bacon drippings.

Roast in a preheated 325°F oven 15 minutes to the pound. When calculating the cooking time for the turkey, do not forget to subtract a pound for the neck and giblets, which are included in the purchase weight. Fifteen minutes can make a big difference, especially with a small bird. A stuffed 25-pound bird will require 6 hours. Baste the turkey occasionally with the reserved bacon drippings and the fat in the pan. Before the vegetables begin to burn, add a little water to the pan. This is often necessary halfway through the roasting.

Brush the turkey with the maple syrup at least 4 times during the last hour of cooking. Test for doneness by piercing the thigh joint with a skewer. If the juices run clear, the turkey is done. An instant-read thermometer should register just under 160°F. Do not forget, as it rests for the requisite 30–40 minutes before carving, the turkey will gain an additional 10–15° from "carryover" cooking. This rest is essential to allow the juices that were driven deep into the center of the meat to flow outward and to relax the meat. This will ensure tender, succulent slices literally oozing with juice. Remove the turkey to a platter and keep warm.

The Sauce

✦ Skim the fat from the roasting pan and discard. Place the pan over medium heat, pour in the cider, and scrape up the browned bits clinging to the pan. Pour the contents of the pan, vegetables and all, into a blender and puree until very smooth. Pour the sauce into a saucepan, bring to a boil, and skim the foam from the surface. Reduce until thickened to your liking, and season to taste with salt and pepper.

Serving
✦ Remove the strings from the turkey and surround with roasted chestnuts and greenery. Carve the turkey at tableside.

Pheasant Roasted with Cepes
Yield 4 servings

Anatomical structure and low fat content make game birds difficult to roast. The breasts of pheasant and ruffed grouse dry out before the legs are cooked. Wrapping them first with rashers of bacon and then grape or cabbage leaves is the traditional way of combatting dryness. Another method is using mushrooms, in this case the wild boletus or cepe, to insulate the breasts from the oven's heat. This technique allows the legs and breasts to finish cooking at about the same time. The mushrooms keep the breasts moist and impart their earthy fragrance into the flesh of the pheasant.

The cepe, a common mushroom, is large in size and beefy in flavor. Almost all its varieties are edible. Novices should consult an experienced mycologist when searching out the wild boletus. Or, purchase dried cepes, reconstitute them, and proceed with the recipe as if using fresh mushrooms.

Serve the delectable birds with wild rice, root vegetables, and a spinach or watercress salad. A fine meal like this deserves an exquisite California Pinot Noir, Merlot, or a French Bordeaux or Burgundy.

2 pheasants, about 2 lb each, dressed
4 large cepes (boletus) wiped clean, stems discarded; or 2 oz dried
    cepes, reconstituted
4 Tbsp butter, melted
Juice 1 lemon
Salt and pepper
1 Tbsp butter fortified with 1 Tbsp vegetable oil for searing

(Continued)

The Sauce

½ cup red wine

1 cup brown stock, canned beef broth, or 1 beef bouillon cube in 1 cup
water

1 Tbsp arrowroot mixed with 3 Tbsp cold water

Salt and pepper to taste

2 Tbsp unsalted butter

✦ *Preheat oven to 350°F.*

When you dress the pheasant, leave the feet attached to make the task
of removing the tendons from the legs a simple matter. With a sharp
knife cut through the skin just into the meat above the knee joint. Snap
the joint, sliding the lower bone sideways from the upper one. Grasp the
drumstick firmly with one hand and the pheasant's foot with your other
hand. Pull the foot free from the bird (this requires some strength). The
tendons will come out with it. Any remaining tendons can be pulled free
with a pair of needlenose pliers. If your pheasants have been purchased
without feet, you can remove all the tendons with a pair of pliers. The
technique of removing the tendons before roasting produces a tender
result unlike the stringy legs of an untreated bird.

Slice the cepes ¼ inch thick and toss in a bowl with the melted butter,
lemon juice, and a bit of salt and pepper. To reconstitute dried mushrooms, immerse them in water in a saucepan. Cover tightly, bring to a
boil, and remove from the heat to soak for 30 minutes. Discard the tough
stems and proceed as for fresh ones.

Loosen the skin over the breasts by running your fingers between the
flesh and the skin, being careful not to pierce the skin. Place the sliced
cepes in a single layer over the breast and pull the skin over the mushrooms. Season the body cavities with salt and pepper. Truss the birds
securely with cotton butcher's twine.

Melt the 1 tablespoon butter over a medium flame in a skillet. Fortify
the butter with an equal amount of vegetable oil so that it does not burn.
Sear the birds until they are nicely browned on all sides and place them
breast side up on a wire rack in a roasting pan.

Roast in a preheated 350°F oven 20 minutes to the pound; average
2-pound birds will take 40 minutes. The pheasants should still be slightly
pink on the bone when done. Test for doneness by piercing the thickest

part of the thigh with the tine of a meat fork. If the juices run clear, the meat is done. Remove to a serving platter to rest for 20 minutes before carving.

The Sauce

✦ Place the roasting pan over a burner set on medium heat. Add the wine and scrape up the browned bits clinging to the pan. Pour this pan sauce into a saucepan. Add the brown stock and reduce by one-third. Mix the arrowroot and cold water in a small bowl until completely dissolved. Stir it into the simmering sauce until thickened and smooth. Swirl in the butter, season to taste with salt and pepper, and strain into a warmed sauceboat.

To Serve

✦ Remove the strings from the birds and carve at tableside since this is an unusual and dramatic presentation. Give each person half a pheasant.

Herbed Chicken Cutlets
Yield 6 servings

Buttermilk keeps these cutlets moist and adds a subtle tang. Accompany with lemon wedges or a cruet of herb-flavored vinegar for a piquant contrast. Serve with rice, broiled tomatoes, a green vegetable, and a salad of butter lettuces.

1½ lb boneless chicken, skin and sinews removed, in ½-inch dice
1 cup buttermilk
¾ cup fine stale bread crumbs plus crumbs as needed for dredging the
   cutlets
1½ tsp salt
⅛ tsp pepper, freshly ground
1 egg
4 Tbsp mixed fresh herbs, chopped fine. Some herbs are more domi-
   nant than others. An herb such as tarragon, thyme, fennel, or rosemary should not make up more than 1 Tbsp of the total mixture.
2 Tbsp butter and 2 Tbsp vegetable oil for browning

(Continued)

✦ Soak ¾ cup bread crumbs in the buttermilk for at least 5 minutes. Puree the chicken cubes in a food processor; add the salt, pepper, and soaked bread crumbs, and process until smooth. Add the egg, run the machine until incorporated, and turn this mousse into a bowl. Cover and refrigerate for 1 hour. A chilled mixture is easier to handle.

Coat your hands with vegetable oil and divide the chicken mousse into 6 equal mounds. Shape them into oblong patties about ¾ inch thick. Roll the cutlets in bread crumbs, patting the crumbs to ensure their adhesion. If you are not going to cook the cutlets immediately, refrigerate until ready to cook.

Preheat oven to 400°F.

Melt 2 tablespoons butter in a skillet over medium heat and add an equal amount of vegetable oil to fortify it. Lightly brown the cutlets on both sides and arrange in a single layer in a baking dish. Bake in a preheated 400° oven 12–15 minutes. The cutlets are done when firm to the touch. Serve immediately.

Summer Succotash with Chicken
Yield 6 servings

Succotash has evolved from a several-course meal into a dish somewhere between a stew and a chowder. A dish that changes with the seasons, its only fixed parts are corn and legumes. Generally a winter succotash contains shell beans as well as corn. These can be cooked with any number of ingredients including potatoes, parsnips, turnips, and carrots, with fresh beef brisket, ham, chicken, pickled pork, or corned beef.

This summer version features chicken, fresh peas, chives, and sweet corn cooked with cream. Served over buttermilk biscuits, it is topped with crisp crumbled bacon.

The Chicken

One 4-lb chicken
2 stalks celery, sliced
1 medium onion, sliced
1 bay leaf
½ tsp black peppercorns
2 sprays fresh thyme or 1 tsp leaf thyme

Small handful fresh parsley
Juice 1 lemon
6 cups cold water

The Succotash

½ lb bacon, ¼-inch dice
2 tsp rubbed (ground) sage
Pinch cayenne
Good grating fresh nutmeg
6 Tbsp all-purpose flour
3 cups chicken stock, canned chicken broth, or 3 bouillon cubes in
   3 cups water
2 cups peas, freshly shelled
2 cups corn, freshly cut
2 Tbsp fresh chives, chopped
1 cup heavy cream
Salt and pepper to taste
One recipe buttermilk biscuits (see Chapter 8, Breads and Breakfast
   Cakes: Buttermilk Biscuits)

The Chicken

✦ Remove the fat from the cavity of the chicken and discard. Place the
chicken in a pot with the vegetables, herbs, spices, lemon juice, and
water. Bring to a boil, reduce to a simmer, and cook covered for 45
minutes. Test for doneness by piercing the thickest part of the thigh with
a skewer; if the juice runs clear, the meat is done. If you are using a
stewing fowl, allow twice as much time for the cooking; make sure the
fowl is tender before removing it. Remove the chicken to a bowl and
allow it to cool for easy handling.

Pick the meat from the carcass, breaking it into bite-size pieces. Strain
the cooking liquid from the chicken into a saucepan and reduce it to 3
cups, about 20–30 minutes.

The Succotash

✦ Cook the bacon in a pot over low heat until crisp. Remove with a
slotted spoon, drain on absorbent paper, and reserve. Add the onions
and sage to the bacon drippings and cook slowly until the onion has

softened. Sprinkle the flour over the onions and stir to a paste. Cook for a few minutes until the paste loses its shine, stirring occasionally. Add 1 cup of the chicken stock and stir until smooth. Increase the heat to medium and add the remaining stock, the cream, the cayenne, and the nutmeg. Simmer slowly for 20 minutes. Add the peas, corn, chicken, and chives and simmer for 10 minutes. Season to taste with salt and pepper.

Ladle the succotash over split buttermilk biscuits. Top with the bacon and a generous grinding of black pepper.

Pot-Roasted Chicken with Cracklings
Yield 4–6 servings

Memories of my grandmother's cooking are few. Her Welsh heritage and the need to make ends meet during the depression encouraged a bland cooking style. However, she did have one triumph that went by the humble name of "pot-roasted chicken." The bird would emerge from the slightly dented pot, plump and beautifully brown, smothered in gravy, with crisp cracklings sprinkled over the top. The vegetables, cooked with the chicken, were essential to the dish. Serve this homey meal with hot rolls or biscuits and mugs of cider.

The Chicken

One 4-lb roasting chicken
½ lb fat salt pork, rind removed
8 small white onions, peeled
4 medium carrots, peeled and halved
4 medium parsnips, peeled and halved
8 small potatoes, peeled
8 cloves garlic, peeled
Several sprigs parsley
2 bay leaves

The Sauce

4 Tbsp rendered chicken fat
3 Tbsp all-purpose flour
The stock from cooking the chicken

1½ cups milk
Pinch cayenne pepper
Good grating fresh nutmeg

The Chicken

✦ *Preheat oven to 325°F.*

Rinse the chicken with cold water and pat dry with a cloth. Remove excess fat from the chicken's body cavity and reserve for the sauce. Season the cavity with salt and pepper and place the bay leaves and parsley inside. Truss the bird with cotton butcher's twine.

Cut the salt pork into strips about 2 inches long as thin as possible. Heat a Dutch oven over low heat and cook the salt pork until crisp. Remove with a slotted spoon, drain on absorbent paper, and reserve. Pour off all but 2 tablespoons of the drippings, increase the heat to medium, and brown the chicken on all sides; remove it to a plate.

Prepare the vegetables as directed. Cut an X into the root end of the onions with the point of a knife to prevent them from falling apart during cooking. Add the vegetables to the pot and roll them around until they shine from the salt pork. Place the chicken on top of the vegetables, breast side down, cover tightly, and place in the preheated 325° oven. Cook 20 minutes to the pound, turning the chicken breast side up halfway through the cooking. Test for doneness by twisting the drumstick. The chicken is done if the drumstick twists free from its socket.

Place the chicken on a serving platter, remove the strings, and surround it with the vegetables and cracklings. Cover and keep warm while making the sauce.

The Sauce

✦ Render the reserved chicken fat in a saucepan over low heat. Add the flour, stir to a paste, and cook for a few minutes until the paste loses its shine. Slowly pour the stock from the pot into the saucepan, stirring as you do so. When smooth, add the milk, nutmeg, and cayenne. Bring to a boil, stirring all the while. Lower the heat slightly and reduce the sauce until thickened to your liking. Season to taste with salt and pepper. Pour into a warmed sauceboat and pass at the table. The chicken requires a resting period of at least 20 minutes before carving, which is more than enough time to make the sauce.

Rabbit Pâté

Yield 1 medium-size pâté

The contrast between the lightly colored rabbit, the violet liver, and the black prunes creates a distinguished presentation. This visual impact can be employed to beautiful effect when displayed on a cold buffet or when presented as a single slice, ungarnished, as an appetizer. Serve with pickled chanterelles, little tarragon pickles, onion marmalade, crusty bread, and a chilled Riesling or champagne.

One 2½–3 lb rabbit, dressed weight, bones removed, all but loins in
  1-inch dice
Butter to sauté the rabbit loins
1 lb pork butt or shoulder, in 1-inch dice
1 lb fresh fatback, in 1-inch dice
The rabbit liver plus 4 duck or chicken livers
8 prunes, pitted and quartered
⅓ cup applejack or brandy
½ cup fresh white bread crumbs
½ cup heavy cream
1 egg plus 2 yolks
1 apple, peeled, cored, and grated
1½ Tbsp kosher salt
1 tsp rubbed (ground) sage
1 tsp leaf thyme
½ tsp nutmeg, freshly grated
½ tsp allspice, ground
Pinch ground cloves
½ tsp black pepper, freshly ground
12 strips bacon
6 bay leaves
Parchment paper and aluminum foil

✦ Place the prunes in a bowl with the liquor and reserve. Toss the pork and fatback cubes with the cubed rabbit meat and pass the meats through the coarse (¼-inch) disc of a meat grinder; run an electric machine at low speed.

Melt the butter in a skillet and sauté the rabbit loins and livers until the loins are barely firm to the touch. Remove from the heat and reserve. In a separate bowl combine the bread crumbs, heavy cream, eggs, grated apple, herbs, spices, and salt.

Using a wooden spoon blend together the ground meats, prunes, liquor, and the bread crumb mixture. Line a 2-quart loaf pan with the bacon strips so that the ends touch on the bottom. Spoon in the pâté until the mold is half full. Place the reserved loins down the center. Cut the livers in half and place a row of them down either side of the loins. Fill with the remaining pâté mixture, making sure that there are no air pockets. Tap the pan on the counter to settle the mixture and to release any hidden air bubbles. Fold the bacon over the pâté and place the bay leaves on top.

Preheat oven to 350°F.

Cut a piece of parchment paper to fit on top of the pâté. Cover the pan with aluminum foil, shiny side down, leaving a little headroom for the pâté to expand during cooking. Cut a few vent holes in the foil to allow steam to escape. Place the pâté in a larger pan filled with water so that the water comes part way up the sides of the pâté mold.

Bake in a preheated 350°F oven for 2 hours. The pâté is done when it reaches an internal temperature of 155°. Remove the foil from the mold and cool the pâté at room temperature for 1 hour, then wrap the pâté, still in the pan, with plastic wrap. Place a piece of wood or a loaf pan of the same size on top of the pâté. Place a 2-pound weight (2 cans of food) on top and refrigerate for at least 24 hours; 48 hours is better. This period will improve the flavor and compress the structure, making the pâté easier to slice.

To unmold the pâté, remove the plastic wrap and place the mold in a pan of warm water to melt the surface fats that adhere the pâté to the mold. Invert the pan and remove the pâté. Wipe the surface with a cloth to remove the natural gelatin and cooking juices and discard the bay leaves.

The pâté is now ready to be sliced and served or partially sliced and arranged around the remaining loaf with condiments for display on a buffet.

Red Meats and Duckling

✦

Roast Leg of Venison with Ginger and Lemon

Venison Chili

Venison and Mushroom Pie

Venison Pâté

Harrington Ham Glazed with Apple Butter and Mustard

Pork Liver Pâté

Smoked Pork Chops with Devil Sauce

Molasses-Glazed Duckling with Cranberry Pear Sauce

Lamb Steaks with Cracked Peppercorns and Currant Jelly

Saddle of Lamb Stuffed with Spinach and Mushrooms

Spit-Roasted Spring Lamb

Beefsteaks Braised with Onions and Ale

Pot-Roasted Beef with Gingersnaps

Calf Liver with Bacon, Tarragon, and Cider Vinegar

Vermont cooking traditions have developed over the centuries by melding the cooking styles of several countries. In the 1600s and 1700s French pioneers entered northern Vermont from Canada, settling among native Abenaki Indians. By the mid-eighteenth century a trickle of English and Scottish settlers moved northward from an overcrowded Connecticut, clearing forests for farmland. After the American Revolution, immigration increased dramatically as war veterans were granted lands in the northern wilderness. The mills and railroads of the mid-nineteenth century attracted French Canadians and Irish. Later in that century, granite and marble quarries drew northern Italians, and the burgeoning railroad systems attracted southern Italians.

Through the 20th century Vermont, as elsewhere in America, has assimilated peoples of strikingly different origins. Ethnic distinctions fade with time, while new ideas continue to flow in and out of Vermont. The legacy of the groups who have lived among the Green Mountains can be traced through various cooking styles.

Venison and Mushroom Pie points to the strong French Canadian influence in Vermont cooking. Beefsteaks Braised with Onions and Ale suggests English roots. Spit-Roasted Spring Lamb is basted with a southern Italian mixture of olive oil, garlic, and herbs. Venison Chili demonstrates that Vermont cuisine is not static—new ideas continue to shape its way of life.

About Red Meats

I have grouped beef, venison, lamb, liver, and duckling together as red meats that can be served roasted "rare." Ham and smoked pork chops require thorough cooking, but seem more at home in this section than with white meats. Corned beef, like ham, should be cooked completely through. I hesitate to use the term "well-done" since it suggests meat overcooked to dry toughness.

When roasting venison, both wild and farm-raised, I suggest a temperature lower than that used for beef and lamb. Venison is very lean, the fat replaced naturally by water. Even moderate oven temperatures (350°–375°F) can result in drying out venison. Strips of bacon or thin sheets of pork fat laid on the meat's surface will help protect it during cooking.

Ham is extremely dense and thus necessitates a low roasting temperature (300°–325°F) to prevent the development of a leathery exterior. Duckling should be roasted at 350° rather than the hotter temperatures that are often suggested, because of its fat content. The technique of slow roasting will sweat the fat from the duckling while ensuring a crisp skin. Duckling can also be prepared by separating the parts, slow-roasting the legs and thighs, and grilling or frying the breast until rare. Each person is served a crisp-skinned thigh and leg and sliced rare breast meat. The carcass and wing sections can subsequently be used for savory soups and stews.

All roasts require a resting period after removing them from the oven, before slicing. During roasting, heat drives the juices into the center of the meat. This is why a roast, sliced directly after being taken from the oven, gives up its juices onto the carving board, the sliced meat showing a gray color with a raw-looking center; 20–30 minutes of resting will relax the muscle fibers, create the process of "carry-over cooking" (which raises the internal temperature an additional 10°–15°), and ultimately yield tender, rosy-colored slices.

Always slice meat across the grain; thinner butcher's cuts, such as flank steak, should be carved across the grain on the bias for larger, more tender slices. Meat cut with the grain will be tough and stringy. Steaks or London broil, which will be served sliced, require a resting period of 10 minutes before carving. Knowing that the meat needs this resting period, remove it from the heat cooked just slightly less than you wish to serve it. It will continue to cook just a little more from steam trapped underneath it.

Meats such as liver, chops, and steaks that are not to be served sliced should also be cooked a little under the desired serving temperature. Steam trapped underneath a piece of grilled or fried meat will continue to cook it for a few minutes. A steak cooked to "medium-rare" will steam to "medium" on a plate if not served immediately. Even so, allow yourself the leisure of not having to chase everyone to the table to prevent the meal from overcooking.

Meat can be marinated for a few hours or even days before cooking to enhance its flavor. Marinades generally contain an acidic agent such as wine, vinegar, or lemon juice. Because of this acidity, avoid the use of aluminum or iron pans. The acids attack the metal, which adversely affect the flavor of the meat, not to mention the questionable effects it could have on human anatomy. Use ceramic, glass, plastic, or stainless steel pans for marinating. Wipe marinated meat dry before cooking; the marinade is often used as the base for sauces.

Stewing meats come from parts of the animal that are worked the hardest. Tenderest cuts come from those that are little exercised. Stewing meats need a slow, moist cooking process. Attempts to decrease the cooking time by raising the heat will only render the meat dry and stringy. Meats that are browned before stewing—searing in the juices—will yield a richer flavor.

Roast Leg of Venison with Ginger and Lemon
Yield 12–15 servings

The flavor of the meat is enhanced with a light marinade, the base for the accompanying sauce. A large roast, this venison is perfect holiday fare.

Slice the venison into large thin slices, cutting perpendicular to the grain of the meat. Arrange the rosy slices of venison on a large platter with red potatoes roasted with spruce boughs, green beans, and sautéed mushrooms. This is a meal on a grand scale and deserves a huge wine to go with it. Serve a robust California Cabernet Sauvignon, Merlot, or a fine Bordeaux or Burgundy.

> 10–12 lb leg venison (weight is calculated for a leg with the shank attached and the aitchbone removed). Venison roasts are best cut from young deer whose meat is tender.
> 1 lb salt fatback, rind removed, sliced into thin sheets; sliced bacon can be substituted

The Marinade

> 1½ cups white wine
> ½ cup lemon juice (juice of 2–3 large lemons)
> ½ cup vegetable oil
> 1 inch ginger root, peeled and sliced thin
> 1 tsp black peppercorns, cracked
> 1 bay leaf, crumbled
> 1 tsp leaf thyme
> Handful fresh parsley, chopped

The Sauce

6 Tbsp butter
1 medium onion, peeled and chopped fine
1 stalk celery, chopped fine
1 tsp black peppercorns, cracked
6 Tbsp all-purpose flour
The Marinade
6 cups brown stock, canned beef broth, or 6 beef bouillon cubes in
   6 cups water
4 Tbsp quince, gooseberry, or currant jelly

The Venison

✦ Remove all fat from the leg. Cut out the gland (lymph node) behind the kneecap. Encased in a hard piece of fat about the size of a quarter, it will impart a bitter taste to the surrounding meat if it is not extracted. Wipe the meat dry and place in a shallow pan. Combine all the marinade ingredients in a bowl, whisk together, and pour over the venison. Do not use an aluminum pan, for the aluminum will react to the acidity of the marinade, creating an off-taste both to the meat and to the sauce made from the marinade. Cover with plastic wrap and refrigerate for 24 hours. Turn the leg over every few hours.

Preheat oven to 325°F.

The next day, wipe the leg dry and lay the sheets of fat or strips of bacon all over the meat. The leg should be removed from the refrigerator about 1 hour before roasting so that it is not ice cold when you put it in the oven. Truss well with cotton string. Place the leg on a wire roasting rack in a large pan and put it on the center shelf of a preheated 450°F oven. Cook for 15 minutes. Reduce the heat to 325° and roast 15 minutes to the pound for a rare roast, 17 minutes per pound for medium rare, and 20 minutes per pound for medium. A 10-pound leg will take 2¼–3¼ hours depending on the desired doneness. An instant-reading meat thermometer, inserted into the thickest portion of the leg, will show 110° for rare, 120° for medium rare, and 130° for medium.

Remove from the oven and discard the strings and fat. Allow the venison to rest 20–30 minutes before carving to enable the juices to redistribute themselves throughout the roast and relax the meat.

(Continued)

The Sauce

✦ Make the sauce while the roast is in the oven. Melt the butter in a saucepan over medium heat. Cook the vegetables slowly until they are lightly colored. Sprinkle the flour over the vegetables, stir to a paste, and cook slowly for a few minutes until the paste loses its shine. Add the marinade and cracked peppercorns and stir until smooth. Pour in the brown stock and bring to a boil. Simmer slowly until the volume is reduced by two-thirds. Strain the sauce through a wire sieve into another saucepan and return to the heat. Adjust the consistency with water, stir in the jelly, and salt to taste. Pour into a warmed sauceboat and pass at the table.

Venison Chili
Yield 6–8 servings

Chili has come into its own in Vermont, a welcome après-ski meal after a day on the slopes. This version, made with venison, uses the tougher cuts and is mildly spiced with some familiar staples from the larder.

Serve the chili piping hot with frosty mugs of beer, bowls of finely chopped raw onion, grated sharp Cheddar cheese, sour cream, and johnnycake. Each person can dress the chili to his or her own liking. A dish of hot pepper relish, served as a condiment, will add the heat for those individuals who like their chili extra spicy. (For johnnycake see Chapter 8, Breads and Breakfast Cakes: Vermont Johnnycake; for hot pepper relish, see Chapter 7, Preserves and Condiments: Hot Pepper Relish.)

½ lb bacon, in ¼-inch dice
2 lb stewing venison, trimmed, in ½-inch dice; beef or lamb may be
   substituted
All-purpose flour as needed for dredging the meat
1 cup onion in ¼-inch dice
4 garlic cloves, minced
2 Tbsp chili powder

¼ tsp cayenne pepper
1 tsp cumin seeds, toasted in a skillet until fragrant and crushed in a
  mortar
1 Tbsp oregano
1 bay leaf
2 cups tomatoes, chopped; or a 1-lb can whole tomatoes, seeded and
  chopped
One 12-oz bottle of beer
2 cups brown stock or beef broth
4 cups cooked kidney beans; rinse if using canned
Salt and pepper to taste

✦ Using a heavy pot, cook the bacon over low heat until crisp, remove with a slotted spoon, and reserve. Do not use an iron pot, for the acidity in this recipe will combine with it to create an off-taste. Toss the meat with the flour, coating it lightly. Increase the heat to high and brown the meat in small batches, adding more fat to the pot if necessary. Remove each batch of browned meat from the pot and reserve. Lower the heat and slowly cook the onion, garlic, herbs, and spices until the onion is translucent. Add the tomatoes, beer, brown stock, and the reserved bacon and meat. Bring to a boil and reduce the heat so the mixture slowly simmers.

Cook the chili, uncovered, for 3 hours. Add water to the pot if it has evaporated too quickly. It takes a long time to tenderize tougher cuts of game. The cooking time can be cut in half if you want to substitute beef or lamb for the venison. Add the beans when the meat is tender and simmer for 30 more minutes. Season to taste with salt and pepper, bearing in mind the saltiness of the bacon. Adjust the consistency as required and serve piping hot.

Chili is one of those dishes that always seems to be better the next day. This is to your advantage since you will undoubtedly want to reheat something already made after a day spent outdoors.

Venison and Mushroom Pie

Yield 6–8 servings

Until recently, only successful hunters could look forward to enjoying this savory game pie. Now, both domestic and New Zealand venison is stocked in butcher's cases at major supermarkets. Apple cider and vinegar combine with mushrooms and venison in the subtly sweet-and-sour filling topped with a flaky golden crust. Serve with a green vegetable, cranberry apple conserve, and a rich dark beer, apple cider, or full-bodied red wine such as Cabernet Sauvignon. Or, look for a fruit wine such as blueberry or pear to complement this wonderful dish.

The Filling

1½ lb stewing venison, trimmed, in ½-inch dice, or leftover roasted venison
1 lb salt pork or slab bacon, rind removed
Water to cover salt pork
Flour as needed to dredge the venison
2 cups onions, diced fine
2 cloves garlic
1 tsp leaf thyme
2 tsp rubbed (ground) sage
3 Tbsp fresh parsley, chopped
1 bay leaf
3 Tbsp all-purpose flour
½ cup cider vinegar
½ tsp black peppercorns, cracked
1½ cups sweet cider
2 cups brown stock, canned beef broth, or 2 beef bouillon cubes in 2 cups water
3 Tbsp butter
1 lb mushrooms, quartered

The Crust

2 cups all-purpose flour
¾ tsp salt
5 Tbsp unsalted butter, chilled
5 Tbsp lard or shortening, chilled

4 Tbsp cold water
1 egg, beaten with 1 Tbsp water

The Filling

✦ Cover the salt pork with water, bring to a boil, and simmer for 10 minutes. Remove from the water, cool to room temperature, and cut into ½-inch cubes. Heat a heavy pot over low heat and fry the salt pork until golden brown. Remove with a slotted spoon and reserve.

Dredge the venison with flour, coating it lightly. Increase the heat to high and brown the venison in small batches in the fat rendered from the salt pork. Remove the venison as it is browned and reserve. Reduce the heat, add more fat if necessary, and add the onions, garlic, thyme, and bay leaf. Cook until the onions just start to take on color. Sprinkle the flour over the onions and stir to a paste. Cook over low heat for a few minutes until the paste loses its shine.

Add the vinegar and peppercorns, stir until smooth, and add the cider, brown stock, venison, and salt pork. Bring this mixture to a boil and simmer slowly for 2 hours, adding more liquid if necessary. The venison should be tender and the sauce thickened. Discard the bay leaf.

Melt the butter in a skillet and sear the mushrooms quickly over high heat. Add to the venison and season to taste. The filling should be just a little thinner than you would want to serve. This will allow for some evaporation as the pie cooks.

The Crust

✦ Sift together the flour and salt into a bowl. Cut the butter and lard into small pieces. Work into the flour using a fork or pastry cutter until the mixture resembles cornmeal. Add the water and work quickly into the flour. Knead the pastry with your fingertips until it will just hold together. Cover with plastic wrap and refrigerate for 1 hour.

Preheat oven to 400°F.

Roll out one-third of the pastry on a lightly floured board and cut into a strip 2 inches wide. Place the strip around the rim of a 9–10-inch deep pie-plate. Glue the strip together with a touch of cold water. Roll out the remaining pastry in a round slightly larger than the pie-plate.

Fill the plate with the venison and wet the edge of the pastry with water. Top with the pastry and crimp the edge. Brush with the beaten egg. Cut several vent holes to allow steam to escape during baking.

Bake on the center shelf of a preheated 400°F oven 45–50 minutes, or until nicely browned. Remove from the oven and let rest for 10 minutes before serving.

Cut wedge-shaped pieces of the crust to place on top of the mushrooms and venison.

Venison Pâté
Yield 1 medium-size pâté

An aromatic, auburn-colored pâté punctuated with earthy morels and sweet, dried apricots. Slice thin and serve with cranberry apple conserve, sour tarragon pickles, whole-grain mustard, dark bread, and a full-bodied red wine.

1½ lb venison, trimmed weight, in 1-inch cubes
1 lb pork shoulder or butt, in 1-inch cubes
1 lb fresh pork fat, in 1-inch cubes
2 Tbsp butter
4 cloves garlic, minced
1 medium onion, chopped fine
1 tsp leaf thyme
1 Tbsp tarragon
1 tsp black peppercorns, cracked
½ tsp ground allspice
½ tsp freshly grated nutmeg
1½ Tbsp kosher salt
½ cup brandy
½ cup heavy cream
½ cup fresh white bread crumbs
2 eggs plus one yolk
1 oz dried morels
8 dried apricots, ¼-inch dice
¼ cup white wine
Sheets of fatback, caul fat, or 12 strips of bacon, for wrapping pâté
6 bay leaves

✦ Remove all fat and sinew from the venison and place all the cubed meat and fat in a ceramic or stainless steel bowl. Melt the butter over low heat and slowly cook the onion, garlic, thyme, tarragon, allspice, nutmeg, and pepper until the onion is translucent. Remove from the heat and cool to room temperature.

Toss the meat cubes with the onion mixture and brandy, cover, and refrigerate overnight. The next day, pass the cubes through the coarse (¼-inch) disc of a meat grinder; run an electric model at low speed. Place the ground meats in a bowl and reserve.

Place the morels in a saucepan and cover with water. Cover tightly, bring to a boil, remove from the heat, and leave to steep for half an hour. Drain the morels, rinse well to remove any grit, and discard the tough stems. Chop the morels coarsely and reserve. While the mushrooms are being reconstituted, dice the apricots and place them in a small bowl with the white wine. The morels and apricots could also be prepared when you cube the meats so the next day you just have to grind the meats and assemble the pâté.

Preheat oven to 350°F.

Combine the morels, apricots, heavy cream, bread crumbs, eggs, and salt in a bowl. Combine this mixture with the ground meats, working it with your hands until it is fully blended. Line a 2-quart loaf pan with the thin-sliced fatback, caul fat, or bacon, arranging it so that it will fully encase the pâté. Spoon the pâté mixture into the mold, making sure there are no air pockets present. Fold the fat over the top so that the pâté is completely surrounded. Arrange the bay leaves on the fat and top with a piece of parchment paper cut to fit inside the loaf pan. Cover the pan with aluminum foil, shiny side down, leaving some headroom since the pâté will expand during cooking. Puncture the foil in several places with the point of a knife to allow steam to escape.

Place the pâté in a pan of water, just like cooking a custard. Bake in a preheated 350° oven 2–2¼ hours. It is done when it reaches an internal temperature of 155° when tested with an instant-read thermometer. Remove the aluminum foil and cool the pâté at room temperature for 1 hour.

Wrap the pâté still in the loaf pan, with plastic wrap. Place a piece of wood or another loaf pan of the same size on top of the pâté, weighted with a 2-pound weight (2 cans of food), and refrigerate for 3 days. This ripening period will greatly improve the flavor and texture of the pâté.

To unmold the pâté, remove the plastic wrap and place the mold in a pan of hot water. This will melt the surface fats that adhere the pâté to the mold. Invert the mold and remove the pâté. Wipe the surface with a cloth to remove the natural gelatin, and discard the bay leaves. Use a sharp, long, thin knife to slice the pâté. The slices can be served and garnished individually as a first course or fanned out and displayed proudly on a buffet.

Harrington Ham Glazed with Apple Butter and Mustard

Vermont's Harrington ham (hams and other Harrington products can be ordered from: Harrington's, Main Street, Richmond, Vermont 05477) is sweet-cured in a brine flavored with maple sugar and then smoked over smoldering corncobs. Thick-cut slices are fork tender, fine of texture, and decidedly not salty. A sauce is unnecessary because the meat is naturally juicy. An apple butter and mustard glaze complements the ham's rich, smoky flavor and makes a beautiful presentation. Serve with maple-baked beans, coleslaw, glazed carrots, pickled green tomatoes, steamed brown bread, and a spicy chutney or conserve.

An uncooked Harrington ham (an uncooked ham will always be juicier than one that is merely reheated)
1 cup sweet cider
1 cup apple butter
4 Tbsp Dijon mustard

✦ *Preheat oven to 300°F.*

The ham should be removed from the refrigerator about 1 hour before cooking so that it is not ice cold when you put it in the oven. Place the ham, flat side down, on a wire rack in a roasting pan. Bake, uncovered, in a preheated 300° oven, basting frequently with cider for 1 hour. Tent loosely with aluminum foil and cook 30 minutes to the pound. A 14-pound ham will require 7 hours total cooking time.

Remove the ham from the oven 1 hour before it is done. Discard the foil and score the fat diagonally in a checkerboard pattern at 1-inch intervals. Return to the oven, uncovered, for half an hour so the scores open up. Increase the oven temperature to 425°F. Blend together the apple butter and mustard. Spread the ham with this mixture, forcing it into the slits. Return the ham to the oven for the final 30 minutes.

The ham is done when it reaches an internal temperature of 155°. The glaze will have started to caramelize, producing a sienna-colored translucent coating that enhances the beauty of the ham. Allow the ham to rest for at least 30 minutes before carving so that the juices can redistribute themselves and relax the meat. As the meat rests, "carryover cooking" will bring the internal temperature up an additional 10–15°. This incredible ham always brings a chorus of oohs and aahs when carved at tableside.

Pork Liver Pâté
Yield 1 large or 2 small pâtés

A country-style pâté that travels well to summer picnics, tastes marvelous at a ski-lunch, or adds a touch of elegance to a buffet. Serve with small sour pickles, onion marmalade, a variety of mustards, crusty bread, and either a full-bodied red wine or a sweet white such as Sauternes.

1 lb pork shoulder or butt, in 1-inch cubes
1 lb veal, in 1-inch cubes
1 lb fresh pork fat, in 1-inch cubes
1½ lb fresh pork liver
¼ cup applejack or brandy
2 Tbsp butter
1 medium onion, chopped fine
4 cloves garlic, minced
2 Tbsp fresh parsley, chopped
1 Tbsp rubbed (ground) sage
2 tsp leaf thyme
½ tsp nutmeg, fresh grated
¼ tsp allspice, ground
¼ tsp cloves, ground
2 Tbsp kosher salt

(Continued)

1 tsp fresh pepper, ground
¾ cup heavy cream
½ cup fresh white bread crumbs
2 eggs, beaten
Sheets of fatback, bacon, or caul fat to wrap pâté
6 bay leaves
Parchment paper to cover pâté
Water for cooking mold

◆ Place the pork, fat, and veal cubes in a bowl and sprinkle with the applejack; cover and refrigerate while assembling the remaining ingredients. Melt the butter in a skillet over low heat and cook the onion, garlic, parsley, sage, and thyme leaves without letting the mixture take on color. Remove from the heat and allow to cool. Mix the heavy cream, eggs, bread crumbs, spices, salt, and cooked vegetables together in a bowl. Puree the liver in a food processor and add to the cream mixture.

Pass the chilled, cubed meats through the coarse (¼-inch) disc of a meat grinder; run an electric machine at low speed. Combine the ground meat with the liver mixture and work with a wooden spoon until the two mixtures are fully blended.

Preheat oven to 325°F.

Line a 2-quart loaf pan or two smaller pans with thin-sliced fatback, strips of bacon, or caul fat. Arrange these sliced fats so that they will overlap on the bottom and top of the pâté. Spoon the pâté into the lined mold, making sure there are no air pockets present. Fold the fat over the top so that the mixture is fully encased.

Arrange the bay leaves on the pâté. Top with a piece of parchment paper cut to fit inside the pan. Cover the loaf pan with aluminum foil, shiny side down, leaving some room for the pâté to expand during cooking. Puncture the foil in several places with the point of a knife to allow steam to escape.

Place the pâté in a pan of water to come about halfway up the sides of the mold and bake in a preheated 325°F oven. Cook 2½ hours for a large pâté and about 2 hours for smaller ones. Replenish the water if necessary during cooking. The pâté is done when an instant-read thermometer reveals an internal temperature of 155°.

Remove the aluminum foil and cool for 1 hour at room temperature. Wrap the pâté, still in the mold, with plastic wrap. Place a piece of wood or a loaf pan of the same size on top of the pâté and weight it with a 2-pound weight (2 cans of food) and refrigerate for at least 24 hours and preferably 48 hours before serving. This storage period will ripen the pâté and compress its structure, thereby making it easier to slice.

To unmold the pâté, remove the plastic wrap. Place the mold in a pan of hot water. This will melt the surface fats that adhere the pâté to the mold. Invert the mold and remove the pâté. Wipe the surface with a cloth to remove the natural gelatin and discard the bay leaves. Slice the pâté thin.

Smoked Pork Chops with Devil Sauce
Yield 6 servings

Tangy devil sauce accents cured and smoked pork chops that are sautéed, flambéed with rum, and bathed in maple syrup. Serve with mashed potatoes mixed with dill or cabbage pancakes and glazed carrots.

The Sauce

2 Tbsp butter
¼ cup onion, chopped fine
2 Tbsp all-purpose flour
¼ cup cider vinegar
2 cups brown stock, canned beef broth, or 2 beef bouillon cubes in 2 cups water
2 tsp Dijon mustard
2 Tbsp sour pickles, chopped fine
2 tsp lemon juice
Pinch cayenne pepper
Salt to taste

The Pork Chops

1–2 smoked rib chops per person
2–3 Tbsp lard or bacon drippings
4 Tbsp rum
3 Tbsp maple syrup

The Sauce

✦ Prepare the sauce before cooking the chops and keep warm or reheat for service. Melt the butter over low heat in a saucepan and cook the onion slowly until translucent. Sprinkle in the flour, stir to a paste, and cook until the paste loses its shine. Pour in the vinegar and stir again to a smooth paste. Add the brown stock, stir well, and increase the heat to medium. Skim the foam from the surface as the sauce cooks. Simmer the sauce until it reduces by half and thickens.

Remove from the heat and add the lemon juice, mustard, diced pickles, and cayenne. Stir until combined and correct the seasoning if necessary. Pour into a warm sauceboat and pass at the table.

The Chops
✦ Melt the lard or bacon drippings in a heavy skillet over medium-high heat. When hot, add the chops and cook 4 minutes on each side. The chops should be nicely browned, cooked through, and firm to the touch. Remove the chops from the pan, pour in the rum, and flambé. When the flame subsides, pour in the maple syrup, return the chops to the skillet, and coat them all over with the syrup. Serve at once.

Molasses-Glazed Duckling with Cranberry Pear Sauce
Yield 4 servings

This roasting technique was passed on to me by an old chef who had been raised on a duck farm in Maine. The ducklings have a crispy, lacquered finish and flesh that is sweet and nearly free of fat. Accompany with wild rice, assorted root vegetables, and a spicy Zinfandel wine.

The Ducks
Two 4-lb ducklings
2 small onions, peeled
12 whole cloves
¼ cup molasses
2 Tbsp cider vinegar

The Sauce
½ cup white sugar
2 Tbsp water

¼ cup cider vinegar
1 cup cranberries
4 ripe pears, peeled and cored
2 cups sweet cider
Pinch ground cloves

The Ducks

✦ Rinse the ducks in cool water and pat dry with a towel. Remove the excess fat from the body cavities and season inside with salt and pepper. Turn the ducks breast-side down and plunge a sharp knife through the carcass on either side of the backbone. This will form two openings about 1 inch long through which the fat can drain as the ducks roast.

For birds with crackly, crisp skin, dry them before roasting in front of an electric fan. Set the ducks on a wire rack about a foot away from the fan and run it at low speed until the skin feels like parchment, 2–3 hours. *Preheat oven to 350°F.*

Stick each onion with 6 cloves and place inside the cavities of the ducks. Place the birds breast-side up on a wire rack set over a shallow roasting pan. Roast on the center shelf of a preheated 350° oven for 2 hours.

Mix the molasses and vinegar. Begin basting the ducks with this mixture after the first hour. Brush them all over at 3 intervals to achieve a well-colored finish.

When the ducks are done, discard the onion and keep the ducklings in a warm place until you are ready to serve. They need to rest for 15–20 minutes before serving so that the meat can relax and the juices redistribute themselves throughout the flesh.

The Sauce

✦ Place the sugar and water in a saucepan and cook over low heat about 5 minutes until the sugar has turned the color of chestnuts. Add the vinegar and scrape the bottom of the pan. Reduce this mixture by half. Add the remaining ingredients and cook slowly for 5 minutes until the cranberries have burst and the pears have softened.

Pass this mixture through the fine disc of a food mill. Return the sauce to a saucepan and reduce over medium heat until thickened. This will yield about 1½ cups of sauce and should take a total time of about 20 minutes. Pour into a warmed sauceboat and serve hot.

(Continued)

To Serve the Ducklings

✦ To carve, make an incision down the center of the duck between the breasts. Run the knife down each side of the rib cage. Cut through the joints that hold the wing to the carcass and the thigh to the hip socket.

Place each split duckling on individual plates with the breast facing the front of the plate. Serve at once.

Lamb Steaks with Cracked Peppercorns and Currant Jelly
Yield 4 servings

During the first half of the nineteenth century Vermont was the number one wool producer in the country. Cheap imported wool brought the industry to a halt. A century and a half later the sheep population is on the rise again. Now raised primarily for meat, Vermont lambs are brought to market at a younger age than their western or foreign counterparts. Their diet, no longer limited to forage, is supplemented by grain. The meat is light in color, low in fat, and exceptionally tender.

These lamb steaks have a snappy coating of cracked peppercorns and a buttery sauce flavored with red wine and currant jelly. Serve them along with a gratin of parsnips or baked russet potatoes, a crisp green vegetable, and a light salad of Boston lettuce or watercress. A red wine with finesse would be a good choice to accompany this lush meal.

The Sauce

6 Tbsp butter
1 small onion, chopped fine
¼ cup red wine vinegar
1 cup red wine
4 Tbsp currant jelly
1 Tbsp Dijon mustard

The Lamb

4 lamb steaks, 8–10 oz each, 1 inch thick, cut from the leg
1 clove garlic
Salt for seasoning

4 tsp black peppercorns, cracked
1 Tbsp butter
1 Tbsp vegetable oil

The Sauce

✦ Make the sauce before the steaks are cooked. Keep it warm or reheat for service. Melt 2 tablespoons butter in a saucepan over low heat. Add the onion and cook until softened. Add the vinegar and reduce until there is just a trace of liquid. Pour in the wine, increase the heat, and reduce by two-thirds. Add the currant jelly, stirring until it is melted. Remove the sauce from the heat and swirl in the remaining butter and mustard until smooth. Season to taste and reserve.

The Lamb

✦ You will need a bone saw and a good boning knife if you want to cut the lamb yourself. Otherwise, have your butcher do it for you. Trim away the fat covering the leg and discard. Cut 1-inch thick steaks from the center of the leg, sawing through the bone. These crosscut steaks will have a ring of bone in the center. There are usually 4–5 nice steaks on the leg. The meat remaining on the bone can be used for a savory stew or a hearty soup.

Rub each steak all over with the garlic and season with a little salt. Using a mallet, side of a cleaver, or mortar and pestle, crack the peppercorns and sprinkle them evenly over both sides of the steaks, pressing them so they adhere. Heat the butter and oil in a heavy skillet over medium-high heat. When the fat is hot, add the steaks and cook until pearls of juice appear on the surface. Turn the steaks over and cook until they resist your touch slightly. Beads of juice will appear on the surface of the meat again, indicating that the steaks are rare. Cook for another minute if you prefer medium-rare. At any point during the cooking, if the steaks seem to be burning, reduce the heat at once. The pepper will become bitter if it is scorched. Place the steaks on individual plates. Reheat the sauce without boiling and spoon it over the lamb. Serve at once.

Saddle of Lamb Stuffed with Spinach and Mushrooms

Yield 10–12 servings

A roast for special celebrations or a sumptuous dinner party. The full saddle of lamb contains two loins and two tenderloins with side flaps attached. This cut produces a neat package perfect for stuffing. When sliced, the cross section reveals rosy rounds of lamb surrounded by the dark green of spinach. Accompany this magnificent roast with wild rice, broiled tomatoes, green beans, and an elegant red wine.

4½–5 lb boneless saddle of lamb
¼ lb bacon, in ¼-inch dice
4 cloves garlic, minced
1 medium onion, chopped fine
10 oz fresh spinach
½ lb mushrooms
1 tsp marjoram
1 tsp rubbed (ground) sage
1 tsp leaf thyme
½ tsp fresh nutmeg, grated
1 slice fresh white bread, grated into crumbs
Few grinds of pepper mill

The Lamb

✦ Remove the excess fat from the outside of the saddle. Turn the saddle over and remove the tenderloins, the two narrow strips of meat on top. Remove all the fat underneath the tenderloins and any along the sides of the loins. Trim the flaps so that when folded under they will meet evenly and overlap by an inch or two. Refrigerate until ready to stuff.

The Stuffing

✦ Wash and dry the spinach, removing and discarding the large, tough stems, and reserve. Cook the bacon over a low flame in a large, heavy skillet. When crisp, remove with a slotted spoon and reserve. Add the garlic and onions and cook until softened. Add the mushrooms, herbs, and spices and cook until the liquid from the mushrooms has evaporated. Turn this mixture into a bowl, add the bread crumbs and the reserved bacon.

Return the skillet to the stove. Increase the heat to high and add the spinach all at once. Cook for a couple of minutes, stirring all the while. When the spinach is cooked, but still dark green, turn it into a colander. Press the spinach with the back of a spoon to extract the superfluous water. Add the spinach to the bowl with the mushroom mixture and stir to combine. Season to taste with salt. Let the mixture cool to room temperature before stuffing the lamb.

Assembly and Roasting

✦ Open the saddle like a book; remove the tenderloins. Using half the spinach mixture, put an even layer over the loins. Lay the tenderloins on top of the stuffing. Cover with the remaining stuffing. Fold the flaps over to make a nice, neat package with the stuffing completely enclosed. Using cotton butcher's twine, truss the saddle all around so it will not open during cooking and will retain its shape.

Preheat oven to 425°F.

Use a heavy skillet with an ovenproof handle; an iron skillet is ideal. Heat the pan on the stove until very hot. Sear the lamb all over until well browned. Turn the saddle so that the flaps are down and oven roast for 55–60 minutes. The roast will be rare at the lesser time and medium-rare after an hour. Remove from the skillet and allow the saddle to rest in a warm place for 15 minutes before carving. This will allow the juices to redistribute themselves throughout the roast and give the tensed fibers of the meat a chance to relax.

Using a long, thin carving knife, cut the roast crosswise into slices about 1 inch thick. Carefully lift the slices onto warm plates using a spatula or the side of the carving knife.

Spit-Roasted Spring Lamb
Yield 10–12 servings

The resurgence of lamb production makes it possible to obtain true spring lamb again. Some growers breed a few animals for birth in late December or early January for the Easter lamb market. These fine animals are scarce but can be specially ordered through some butchers. They are always available directly from the grower.

Spring lamb has the characteristics of veal though lamb need not be cooked until well done. Spring lamb is nearly white to pink in color. The nature of the meat derives from its diet of mother's milk. Lambs' live weight runs about 40 pounds, and they dress out to about 50 percent of their standing weight.

Buying lamb from a grower and butchering it yourself guarantees a prime animal. Most growers are family operations with relatively small flocks. Usually they can arrange to have the animal slaughtered and butchered for you. Check the classified ads in your newspaper under "livestock." If you decide to do the relatively simple butchering job yourself, you will gain a beautiful, warm sheepskin.

Serve with assorted vegetables, rice, salad, hot rolls or freshly baked bread, and a fine red wine.

1 spring lamb, about 20 lb dressed weight
2 cups olive oil
4 bay leaves, crumbled
6 cloves garlic, peeled and sliced
1 small onion, peeled and chopped
1 Tbsp rosemary
1 Tbsp thyme
1 Tbsp oregano
1 tsp black peppercorns, cracked
Juice 2 lemons

✦ Prepare the lamb for roasting by removing the hooves and the head. Wire the legs up close to the body. Prepare a roasting pit or an oil drum cut in half lengthwise. Build a good fire with hardwood, allowing it to burn down to charcoal. Add more wood to maintain a low fire. Position the lamb on the spit high enough over the fire so that the flames do not lick at the meat. A slow-turning mechanical or electrically operated spit is recommended; these spits are available through many rental stores.

To make the basting medium, place all the ingredients in a blender and puree until smooth. Baste the lamb at the beginning of the cooking and from time to time during the roasting. Branches of fresh or dried herbs, onions, garlic, corncobs, etc. can be added to the coals during the cooking. Their smoke will add a subtle fragrance to the meat.

Once the meat has started to take on color, rake the fire to the ends of the pit and wrap the narrow central section, the rack and loins, with a double layer of aluminum foil. The fore and aft of the lamb have a greater quantity of meat than the midsection. They require a longer cooking time to obtain the same degree of doneness.

The lamb will take 3½–4 hours depending on its size and the outside temperature. It will require less time on a warm day, more on a cold day. Check for doneness by feeling the thickest portion of meat in the legs and shoulders. When the meat feels springy, but not yet firm, it is done. An instant-read meat thermometer inserted in the thickest part of the legs and shoulders should register 115°F.

Remove the lamb from the spit and let it rest for 20 minutes before carving. The meat will be a delicate pink color and will slice like butter. Carve the lamb by disjointing into the regular butcher's cuts: legs, shoulders, loins, etc. Slice by holding your knife perpendicular to the grain of the meat. Arrange on a heated platter and serve buffet-style.

Beefsteaks Braised with Onions and Ale

Yield 6 servings

A steak and a cold brew is probably the most relished meal in America. Braising in ale tenderizes the beef, imparting the aromatic bitterness of hops and the sweet flavor of malted barley. This warming winter meal of fork-tender beef, with plenty of rich gravy and sweet onions, is just the thing for an informal dinner with friends. Serve with buttermilk biscuits, mashed potatoes, a green vegetable, and a tossed salad. Accompany this meal with mugs of brew or a red table wine.

3 lb bottom round
All-purpose flour for dredging the meat
2 Tbsp butter
2 Tbsp vegetable oil
3 cups onions, sliced thin
1 tsp leaf thyme
¼ tsp ground allspice
¼ cup cider vinegar
One 12-oz bottle light ale or beer
1 cup brown stock, canned beef broth, or 1 beef bouillon cube in 1 cup
    water
2 Tbsp Dijon mustard

✦ Cut the beef into 6 steaks and pound to a thickness of ¼ inch with a mallet. Season with salt and pepper. Dredge the steaks in flour, patting them between your hands to remove the excess.

Preheat oven to 325°F.

Melt the butter with the oil in a heavy skillet. Increase the heat to high and brown the steaks on both sides. Remove the beef to a plate and reserve. Reduce the heat to medium and add the onions, thyme, and allspice. Cook until golden brown, stirring occasionally. Pour in the vinegar to scald. Add the ale and brown stock, bring to a boil, and then remove from the heat.

Ladle half the sauce into a casserole dish with a tight-fitting cover. Spread the tops of the steaks with the mustard and arrange in a single layer in the casserole. Ladle the remaining sauce over them. Cover and bake in a preheated 325° oven for 2 hours or until fork tender.

Remove the steaks to a serving platter and keep warm. Pour the sauce into a saucepan. Skim the fat from the surface and then bring to a boil. Adjust the consistency by reducing or adding liquid as necessary. Season to taste with salt and pepper.

Pour the sauce over the steaks and serve.

Pot-Roasted Beef with Gingersnaps
Yield 8 servings

Pot roasting is an ancient cooking method. Long ago the vessel containing the meat and seasonings would be buried in a hole lined with heated stones, covered with hot coals, and topped with a layer of earth. The "roast" would cook slowly all day with all the flavor sealed in the pot. This old technique is still used for baked beans at hunting camps. This recipe creates a facsimile of the rich, traditional flavors but bows to the ease of modern cooking methods.

Serve with mashed or boiled potatoes, braised red cabbage, assorted root vegetables, and mugs of dark beer, frothy hard cider, or freshly pressed sweet cider.

3½–4 lb beef bottom round or shoulder, trussed
1 Tbsp butter
1 Tbsp vegetable oil
½ tsp black peppercorns, cracked
1 tsp whole allspice, cracked
2 medium onions, peeled and sliced
½ cup cider vinegar
2 Tbsp maple or brown sugar
1 cup sweet cider
½ cup gingersnap crumbs

✦ Pat the beef dry and rub a little salt into it. Lay the cracked spices on a counter and roll the meat in them to give an even coating, massaging them into the beef. Heat the butter and oil in an enameled or lined Dutch oven over medium heat. An iron pot will react to the acidity of the vinegar and adversely affect the flavor. Brown the meat on all sides, being careful not to burn the spices. Remove the meat to a plate. Lower the heat and add the onions. Cook them without coloring. Add the vinegar and sugar and reduce by one-half. Pour in the cider, lay the meat on the bed of onions, and cover tightly.

Cook in a preheated 275°F oven for 2½–3 hours or until the meat is tender. Test for doneness by inserting a 2-pronged meat fork into the roast, which is done when the fork releases easily. Remove the beef to a platter and keep warm. Allow the beef to rest for 20 minutes before slicing.

Pass the gingersnaps through the fine disc of a food mill or put them in a bag and reduce to a powder with a mallet. Skim the fat from the sauce and discard. With the sauce simmering, add the gingersnaps a spoonful at a time until it has thickened. Pour into a blender and puree until smooth. Return the sauce to the pot, adjust the consistency with cider, if necessary, and salt to taste.

Remove the string from the beef and slice thin with the knife held perpendicular to the grain of the meat. Arrange the beef on a platter with a variety of boiled root vegetables around the perimeter. Spoon a little of the sauce over the meat and pass the remainder in a sauceboat.

Calf Liver with Bacon, Tarragon, and Cider Vinegar
Yield 4 servings

Fresh calf liver, quickly sautéed, topped with crunchy bacon, and served up rare is a real treat. Since everyone does not agree on this point, it is best to take a poll before serving this dish. Serve with Straw Potatoes (see Chapter 6, Vegetables) and a crisp green vegetable. A Pinot Noir or Merlot complements this dish nicely.

The Sauce

1 Tbsp tarragon
1 small onion, chopped fine
1 tsp black peppercorns, cracked
½ cup cider vinegar

2 cups brown stock, canned beef broth, or 2 bouillon cubes dissolved in 2 cups water

1 Tbsp cornstarch mixed in a bowl with 3 Tbsp water

The Liver

1¾ lb calf liver, ½ inch thick

8 strips bacon

Flour as needed for dredging the liver

The Sauce

✦ Put the tarragon, onion, peppercorns, and vinegar in a saucepan over low heat and reduce until there is just a tablespoon of liquid remaining. Add the stock and reduce by one-half. Pour the cornstarch and water mixture into the sauce, stirring while you pour. Bring the sauce to a boil and adjust the consistency by adding more liquid or reducing as necessary. The sauce should have the viscosity of heavy cream.

The Liver

✦ Since sliced liver quickly loses its blood, wait until the last minute before you portion the liver. Cook it the day you purchase it from your butcher.

Heat a large iron skillet over medium heat. Cook the bacon until crisp, drain on absorbent paper, and reserve. Dredge the liver with flour and pat it between your hands to remove the excess. Add a little vegetable oil to the pan if there is not enough rendered bacon fat. Increase the heat to high and sear the liver for 2 minutes. Turn over, reduce the heat to medium-high, and cook for a further 3 minutes or so. When pearls of blood appear on the surface and the liver feels slightly springy to the touch, it is rare. Cook for another ½ minute for medium-rare.

Place the liver on individual plates, spoon the sauce over it, and top with the bacon.

Vegetables

✦

Gratin of Parsnips

Fiddleheads with Lemon Butter and Chives

Asparagus Simply Cooked

Baby Beets Cooked with Their Greens

Sweet Corn, Corn Oysters, and Corn Fritters

Coleslaw with Apples and Mustard

Grated Zucchini with Basil

Summer Potato Salad

Glazed Carrots with Apples and Cinnamon

Fried Green Tomatoes

Soufflé of Winter Squash with Roasted Garlic

Cabbage Pancakes

Straw Potatoes

Brussels Sprouts with Orange Butter

Maple-Baked Beans

Roasted Chestnuts

Red Bliss Potatoes Baked with Spruce Boughs

Everything that grows
Holds in perfection but a little moment
William Shakespeare, Sonnet 15 1.1

Fresh vegetables are like cut flowers. They are sweet and delicate only for a very short while. Vegetables that are out of season, canned, or frozen are of no more substance than dried flowers. Though agreeable to the eye, they are without scent or soul. Even with the use of cold frames and cloches, the growing season in Vermont is unmercifully brief. From the last frost in June to the first snows of September, gardeners battle black flies, hail, floods, and drought for those few precious greens, tubers, sprouts, and stalks.

The harvest in Vermont begins at an unlikely time of year. The snows are still deep, the nights well below freezing. As winter begins to lose its grip, the sugar maples are tapped. It can happen before Town Meeting day—the first Tuesday in March—or not until April, you never know. The sweet sap is boiled down to make the syrup that has become synonymous with the state. As the ground thaws, it is time to dig up wintered-over parsnips that have sweetened beneath the icy covering. As the ground starts to warm, rhubarb, spinach, fiddleheads, and chives are among the first edible plants to appear.

Foraging, still a part of rural life, supplements the garden. We collect morels, asparagus, cattail shoots, sorrel, and dandelion greens. Blooming lilacs indicate that the ground is ready for planting, and gardening begins in earnest. As June turns into summer, warm weather encourages wild strawberries, lettuces, and early peas. The direct sunlight of July and August produces the bulk of the crops destined for the jelly cupboard, pantry, and freezer. Luscious berries, chanterelles, herbs, real tomatoes, and fragile summer vegetables create splendid meals on warm, breezy evenings.

As summer slips away, nights are cool enough for two quilts; but the days are still sunny and pleasant. Now sweet corn, my favorite vegetable, comes into season. Roasted over glowing embers or quickly boiled, it is beyond compare. The tiny, tender kernels burst with pure sugar.

With frost warnings the hillsides are alive with color in one grand finale before it is all swept away. Squashes and field pumpkins are collected, onions dried in the sun, and apples pressed into cider. Only Brussels sprouts can take the weather, standing on sentry duty well into November.

Gratin of Parsnips
Yield 6–8 servings

The iciclelike root of the parsnip is well suited to a frigid climate since frost improves the flavor. Parsnips are best if left in the ground and dug up the following spring. Not only does this make them sweeter, but they become the first fresh vegetable of the season. Serve this dish as an alternative to potatoes with pork, poultry, or game.

2 lb parsnips, peeled, trimmed, and sliced
Juice 1 lemon
¼ tsp ground allspice
4 Tbsp butter
Salt and pepper to taste
½ cup chopped walnuts
1 cup grated Cheddar cheese

✦ Place the parsnips in a saucepan of cold water with a pinch of salt and the juice from half of the lemon. Bring to a boil, reduce the heat, and simmer the parsnips until soft, 10–15 minutes. Drain and mash until smooth or pass through a food mill. Add the butter, the remaining lemon juice, and the allspice. Work the mixture until smooth and season to taste with salt and pepper.

Preheat oven to 400°F.

Generously butter a casserole dish, fill with the parsnip mixture, and smooth the top. Toss the walnuts with the cheese and sprinkle on top. Tent the casserole loosely with a piece of aluminum foil. Bake on the center shelf of a preheated 400° oven 35–40 minutes or until the topping is melted and slightly colored. Serve immediately.

Fiddleheads with Lemon Butter and Chives
Yield 6 servings

A poll designed to determine Vermont's "state vegetable" drew unexpected results. Many respondents listed fiddleheads as their choice. The graceful stalks, which make their appearance early in May in wetlands, have a delicate flavor that suggests asparagus.

Ostrich fern fiddleheads are easily identified by the onionskin covering that loosely clings to the emerging scroll-shaped shoots. Because these initial fronds are sterile, there is no danger of damaging the wild plants by overpicking. Fiddleheads are delicious served with sautéed trout, shad roe, and salmon.

4 cups ostrich fern fiddleheads
4 Tbsp unsalted butter
Juice 1 lemon
2 Tbsp fresh chives, chopped
Salt and pepper to taste

✦ Empty your basket of fiddleheads into a sink filled with cold water. Agitate the water with your hands for a minute or two to loosen the onionskin covering on the ferns. Drain the water from the sink and finish cleaning the skins from the fiddleheads under cold running water.

Bring a pot of water to a boil. Drop the fiddleheads into the actively boiling water and cook until crisp-tender, about 6 minutes. When done, drain the brackish cooking liquid and rinse the fiddleheads under cold running water, drain, pat dry, and reserve.

Heat the butter in a skillet over low heat until melted. Increase the heat to high and immediately add the fiddleheads, lemon juice, and chives. Cook until the sauce is thickened to the consistency of cream. If the sauce separates, you can emulsify it by adding a tablespoon of water and swirling it together. Season to taste with salt and freshly ground pepper. Serve immediately.

Asparagus Simply Cooked

Memorial Day signals the beginning of Vermont's asparagus season. You will see this vegetable in supermarkets well before this date, but the sweet native variety that makes its appearance at farmers' markets along with rhubarb and various greens is well worth the wait. Low in calories, high in vitamin C and minerals, this vegetable is as good for you as it is good to eat.

Buying Asparagus

✦ When purchasing asparagus, look for clean, crisp stalks that have survived the passage from field to greengrocer without abuse. Firm, smooth stalks should be green for the greater part of their length. Most commercial asparagus is cut for weight. The inedible portion of the shoot, ranging in color from violet and brown to white, should constitute no more than one-third of the total length. The tips of young, tender stalks are pointed and tightly closed. Thick shoots are just as tender as thin ones; toughness comes only from age. Either the asparagus was picked too late, or it has spent too much time at the market. Do not consider asparagus that is shriveled or limp.

The natural sugar in asparagus, like that in sweet corn, begins to convert into starch soon after the vegetable is picked, so the sooner asparagus is eaten, the better it will be.

If you own even a small plot of land, you should consider planting some asparagus. It is a small investment that will repay itself with interest year after year.

Preparing Asparagus

✦ Lay the asparagus on a counter and grasp it just below the tip. Run a vegetable peeler lightly over the spears to remove the little nubs that are the plant's leaves and the first layer of skin. Then grasp the asparagus at the tip and the tail, and snap it in two. The spear will break at the point where the tender portion joins the tough base. The edible portion is usually 5–6 inches in length.

Bring a large pot of water to a boil. Drop the asparagus into the actively boiling water, in batches, so that the water continues to boil. Cook until crisp-tender, only a minute or two. There is only one sure way to test for doneness; that is, of course, to bite it. When the asparagus is cooked, remove it from the pot with a pair of tongs and plunge immediately into ice water. This will set the color and arrest the cooking. When completely cool, drain the asparagus, cover, and refrigerate until you are ready to serve it.

Serving Asparagus

✦ Two pounds of asparagus (store weight) will yield 4–6 servings. You will need somewhat less if you have harvested it from your own garden. It can be served hot or chilled, by itself, or in combination with countless other foods. It has an affinity for butter, cream, and eggs, especially when united with lemon juice or vinegar to accent its flavor.

To serve asparagus hot, simply reheat the previously blanched spears quickly over medium-high heat with plenty of butter. Season to taste with salt and freshly ground black pepper and finish with a good squeeze of lemon juice. Arrange the spears on a platter and serve immediately. Served chilled, the asparagus can be a light first course or a salad dressed with a vinaigrette flavored with Dijon mustard and fresh herbs.

Baby Beets Cooked with Their Greens
Yield 4 servings

When you buy beets by the bunch, you get two vegetables for the price of one. The sweet, tender roots are a perfect complement to the bitter greens. When purchasing beets, make sure they have been handled properly after picking. They should be held in a pan of cool water to prevent the greens from wilting, as if they were cut flowers. The beets should be firm to the touch, deeply colored, and without splits. Allow 2–3 beets per person depending on the size of the vegetables. Young beets are smaller, more tender, and have a shorter cooking time. Their greens tend to be sweeter as well.

8 beets, golf-ball size
Cold water to cover
The beet greens
2 Tbsp butter
2 Tbsp red wine vinegar
Salt and pepper to taste

✦ Cut the greens from the beets, leaving about ½ inch of stem. Beets larger than a golf ball should be cut in half, top to bottom, so the vegetables will be of a similar size with the same cooking time. Wash the beets and place in a saucepan with cold water to cover.

Put a lid on the pot, bring to a boil, and reduce the heat to a simmer. Cooking time for beets is related to the timespan between harvest and preparation. A small beet pulled from the garden and cooked the same day will be done in 5 minutes. One of a similar size that has been in winter storage for weeks or months will require up to 30 minutes.

Cook until the beets are tender, offering no resistance when pierced with a fork. Plunge the beets into ice water and allow to cool. Slip off the skins, trim the root ends, pat dry, and reserve.

Wash the beet greens thoroughly and trim the stems at the base of the leaves. Slice the stems into 1-inch pieces. Place the leaves and stems in a skillet with ⅛ inch of water. Place the cooked beets on top and dot with butter. Cover the pan and place over medium heat. Once it begins to steam, it will take 3–4 minutes for the greens and stems to be tender and the beets rewarmed. Drain and place the greens and stems on a serving platter, nesting the beets on them. Season with salt and freshly ground pepper and sprinkle with vinegar. Serve at once with a little more butter and vinegar if desired.

Sweet Corn

Sweet corn achieves its full potential in the special climate of northern New England. Warm days nurture the tall green stalks; cool nights prevent the sugar in the corn from converting to starch. The season begins with yellow corn in early August, then Butter and Sugar, and, finally, Silver Queen around Labor Day. The huge ears crowded with tiny white kernels are a long-awaited treat.

A new chapter on sweet corn is being written with the introduction of the "sugar-enhanced" and genetically altered varieties. These new strains of corn will keep for weeks without losing their sugar content and can be grown in hot climates. The main problem with them is that they just don't taste like corn. Science still has a long way to go before the so-called super sweet corn can compare with the delicate flavor of Country Gentleman or Silver Queen.

There are two time-honored methods of preparing green corn: roasted in the husk over a bed of glowing embers or shucked and quickly cooked in boiling water. Both methods provide excellent results, but there is something special about the roasted ears.

Corn Roasted in the Husk

All that is required is a bed of glowing coals, freshly picked corn, a tub of butter, and a shaker of salt. Place the corn on a grill and turn the ears a quarter turn every 2–3 minutes. The grill should be high enough over the coals so the husks slowly turn a golden brown. If flames lick at the ears or if the husks blacken, the grill should be raised. The corn is done when the tassels have burned off and the husks are evenly colored, about 15 minutes. Pile the ears on a platter and serve at once.

Boiled Corn on the Cob

Some recipes call for soaking the corn in milk prior to its cooking. Others suggest adding sugar to the cooking water to refresh old corn. However, corn that has gone by or is starchy can never be brought back. It absolutely must be freshly picked or the sugar will have converted to starch by the time you get it to the pot.

Pick the corn in the cool of the evening and remove the husks and the silk. Fill a large pot one-third full of water and bring to a boil. Do not add salt to the water; salt will toughen the kernels. Add the corn, cover, and cook for 3 minutes, counting from the time the water returns to a boil. Pile the corn onto a platter and serve at once with a good supply of butter and salt.

Corn Oysters and Fritters

Corn oysters and fritters are closely related. The name is determined by their characteristic size and shape rather than by ingredients or method of preparation. Corn oysters are delicate puffs of sweet corn that bear a physical kinship to their aquatic namesakes. When made with grated corn, they are somewhat oysterlike in texture. They need be served only with sweet butter and a peppermill.

Fritters are usually larger, use whole-kernel corn, and can be deep-fried or pan-fried. Their affinity for maple syrup permits the use of starchy or frozen corn.

Corn Oysters
Yield 2 dozen oysters

1 cup corn, grated
4–6 Tbsp all-purpose flour
2 eggs, separated
1 Tbsp bacon drippings or melted butter
½ tsp salt
¼ tsp black pepper, freshly ground
1 Tbsp fresh chives, chopped (optional)
1 inch lard or shortening
½ lb fresh-picked crabmeat (optional)

✦ Using the coarse side of a hand grater, grate enough fresh corn to yield 1 cup. Stir the egg yolks, salt, and pepper into the corn with a fork. Add 4 tablespoons flour and stir into the corn. If any liquid runs out around the edges, add a little more flour. Add the chives if desired and stir in the bacon drippings or melted butter.

In a separate bowl, whip the egg whites with a pinch of salt to soft peaks. Stir a spoonful of the beaten whites into the corn mixture to lighten it. Fold in the remaining whites, carefully, so they will retain their volume. The batter should be thick but light.

Heat 1 inch of lard or shortening in a heavy pot or high-sided skillet over a medium flame. If you have a thermometer, the fat should be kept between 350° and 375°F. Drop level tablespoons of the batter into the fat and deep-fry, a few at a time, until golden brown on both sides. Drain on absorbent paper and keep warm in a low oven while cooking the remaining oysters.

In addition to their use as a vegetable side dish, corn oysters make a popular appetizer. Fresh-picked Maine crabmeat has recently become a reliable staple in the fish market. Add one-half pound of crabmeat to the corn oyster batter and deep-fry as usual. Serve with mustard butter and lemon wedges as a first course, or make a meal of them.

Corn Fritters
Yield 3 dozen fritters

3 cups corn, cut
1 cup all-purpose flour
1 tsp baking powder
½ tsp baking soda
1 tsp salt
Grating fresh nutmeg
¾ cup buttermilk
2 eggs
1 Tbsp bacon drippings or melted butter for pan-frying
1 inch lard or shortening for deep-frying

✦ Stand the ears of corn on end and place the blade of a sharp knife parallel to the cob. Cut the kernels from the cob with a downward stroke. Mix the corn with the eggs, buttermilk, salt, and nutmeg. Sift together the flour, baking powder, and baking soda, and add to the batter, stirring until smooth. Stir in the bacon drippings or butter.

The fritters are usually deep-fried to achieve their characteristic shape, but they may also be pan-fried. Pan-fry them in a heavy skillet over medium flame 2–3 minutes to the side. They should be golden brown and firm to the touch when done.

Deep-fry them in 1 inch lard or shortening over a medium flame. Maintain the temperature of the fat at 350°–375°F. Drop rounded table-spoons of the batter into the fat and cook until golden brown on both sides. Cut one open to make sure you are cooking them all the way through. For best results, the cooked fritters should be about the size of a hen's egg. Drain on absorbent paper and keep warm in a low oven while cooking the remaining fritters. Serve with hot maple syrup with any entrée from ruffed grouse to ham steaks for a famous dinner.

Coleslaw with Apples and Mustard
Yield 12 servings

Coleslaw is so versatile it can be served as a vegetable, salad course, or relish. Although normally relegated to the realm of outdoor summer cookery, it is the perfect foil for cold-weather dishes—baked ham, codfish cakes, roast goose, duckling, and braised meats.

1 medium head of cabbage, to yield about 10 cups of fine-shredded cabbage
1 cup carrot, grated
1 medium onion, grated and squeezed dry in a towel
3 apples, peeled, grated, and squeezed dry in a towel
¼ cup light brown sugar
2 Tbsp cider vinegar
4 Tbsp whole-grain mustard
1 cup mayonnaise
2 tsp salt
1 tsp fresh black pepper, ground

✦ Remove the outside leaves from the cabbage and discard. Slice the cabbage in half from top to bottom and remove the core and the large, tough ribs. Slice the leaves fine and pile them into a colander. Squeeze the cabbage roughly with your hands to extract any superfluous liquid. Toss with the prepared carrots, onion, and apples, and reserve.

In a separate bowl combine the remaining ingredients to make the dressing and stir until smooth. The key to a light, crisp slaw is to dress the cabbage as closely to serving as possible. Toss the cabbage mixture with the dressing, adjust the seasoning to taste, and refrigerate until needed.

Grated Zucchini with Basil

Yield 6 servings

Recipes for summer vegetables reflect the lifestyle of the season. This recipe can be done at the last minute to accompany a barbecue or the contents of a successful angler's creel.

6 zucchinis, each the size of a stick of butter
1 clove garlic, minced
1 Tbsp chopped fresh basil
Pinch crushed red pepper
3 Tbsp butter
Salt and pepper to taste

✦ Wash the zucchinis, wipe them dry, and cut off the ends. Grate them onto a clean towel, using the coarse side of the grater, and wring out the excess moisture. Toss the zucchini in a bowl with the garlic, basil, and red pepper. Melt the butter in a skillet over medium-low heat. Add the zucchini and cover. Cook until it is crisp-tender and has absorbed the butter, about 3 minutes. Shake the pan halfway through the cooking to prevent sticking. Season to taste with salt and freshly ground pepper. Spoon onto a platter and garnish with a bright yellow zucchini blossom.

Summer Potato Salad
Yield 8 servings

The nutlike texture of raw garden peas and spunky, tender mustard greens turns an ordinary dish into a refreshing seasonal offering.

2½ lb waxy potatoes such as Red Bliss or Green Mountain
1 cup raw peas, freshly shucked
1 small onion, diced fine
1½ cups Sharp Cheddar Cheese Salad Dressing (see Chapter 7, Preserves and Condiments)
Salt and freshly ground pepper to taste
Small handful young mustard greens, shredded
1 Tbsp chopped fresh chives

✦ Place the unpeeled potatoes in a pot, cover with cold water, and bring to a boil. Reduce the heat and simmer slowly until the potatoes are tender. Test them with a fork or small pointed knife for doneness. Be careful not to overcook them. Drain the potatoes and peel them while still warm. Refrigerate the potatoes overnight to give them a firm, waxy texture.

Slice the potatoes ¼ inch thick and toss with the onion, peas, and Cheddar cheese dressing. Season to taste with salt and freshly ground black pepper. Just before serving, toss the salad with the shredded mustard greens. Turn the salad into a serving bowl and garnish with the fresh chives.

Glazed Carrots with Apples and Cinnamon
Yield 8 servings

Some main dishes call for a sweetened vegetable to balance the meal. These carrots are well suited to duckling, goose, pork, and pot-roasted meats.

2 lb carrots, peeled and roll-cut, or sliced on the bias
2 cooking apples, peeled, cored, and sliced
3 Tbsp butter
2 Tbsp maple or light brown sugar
½ tsp cinnamon, ground
Salt and pepper to taste

✦ Place the prepared carrots in a pot of cold water, bring to a boil, and cook them uncovered until crisp-tender. Since carrots come in such a variety of shapes and sizes, you must judge the cooking time yourself. Test doneness by fishing a carrot piece out of the boiling water and biting into it. Drain the carrots and plunge them into ice water. You can prepare the carrots up to this point in advance and finish the preparation when you are ready to serve.

Melt the butter in a skillet over medium-high heat. Add the apples and let them color slightly. Add the carrots, shaking them about the pan as they cook. Cook until the apples have softened and the vegetables are hot. Increase the heat to high and add the sugar and cinnamon. Toss the mixture until evenly coated, about 1 minute. Season to taste with salt and pepper and serve immediately.

Fried Green Tomatoes
Yield 4 servings

Fried green tomatoes are so good you may find yourself picking new tomatoes in July for this unusual dish.

8 strips bacon
4 large green tomatoes
Stone-ground cornmeal and all-purpose flour mixed together for dredging the sliced tomatoes
3 Tbsp maple syrup
4 Tbsp cider vinegar
Salt and freshly ground black pepper to taste

✦ Cook the bacon in a skillet over medium-low heat until crisp. Drain on absorbent paper and keep warm. Cut the tomatoes into ¼-inch slices and discard the ends. Salt and pepper the slices and dredge them in the cornmeal-flour mixture. Fry the tomatoes in the bacon fat over medium heat until golden brown on both sides. Shingle the tomatoes on a serving platter and keep warm.

Pour off all but 1 tablespoon of the bacon drippings, add the syrup and vinegar, and scrape up the browned bits from the skillet. Reduce this liquid to a thin syrup and spoon it over the tomatoes. Garnish with the bacon, either crumbled or left whole. Serve immediately.

Soufflé of Winter Squash with Roasted Garlic
Yield 6 servings

Place this savory soufflé in the oven when you remove your glazed ham or turkey. By the time the roast is ready to be sliced, the soufflé will be puffed and golden.

> 2 cups puree of winter squash (see below for method)
> 1 head garlic, unpeeled, separated into cloves
> ½ cup milk
> 4 Tbsp butter
> 1 tsp rubbed (ground) sage
> Grating fresh nutmeg
> Pinch cayenne
> ½ cup grated sharp Cheddar cheese, well packed
> 4 eggs, separated

✦ A small fine-grained squash such as acorn or butternut is recommended for a creamy texture. If using canned squash, simply roast the garlic separately and proceed with the recipe as written. A medium acorn or a small butternut squash should yield about 2 cups; 1 can prepared squash contains 2 cups.

Preheat oven to 350°F.

Butter and flour a 1½-quart soufflé dish and place it in a warm spot until ready to use. Cut the squash in half, scoop out the pulp, and smear the insides with half the butter. Place the garlic in 2 equal piles on a baking pan and cover with the squash. Bake in a 350° oven until soft, 1–1¼ hours. When done, peel the garlic and puree with 2 cups of the squash. Place the squash, seasonings, cheese, and remaining butter in a saucepan. Cook over low heat, stirring all the while, until the butter and cheese have melted into the mixture. Remove from the heat and quickly stir in the yolks. Turn the mixture into a large bowl. Cool to room temperature before proceeding.

Preheat oven to 375°F.

Whip the egg whites with a pinch of salt to soft peaks (do not overwhip). Stir one-third of the whites into the squash to lighten it. Fold in the remaining whites and pile into the prepared soufflé dish. Bake on the center shelf of a preheated 375°oven for 35–40 minutes, or until puffed, golden, and the center is set. Like all soufflés this must be served at once, directly from the oven to the table. Make sure your guests are seated around the table. Once it comes in contact with the cooler air of the room, the soufflé will start to lose volume.

Cabbage Pancakes
Yield 4 servings (12 pancakes)

Serve these crunchy, sweet-and-sour pancakes with braised brisket of beef, corned round, roast duckling, or pork. Top with a dollop of sour cream or applesauce.

2 cups cabbage, shredded fine
1 apple, peeled and grated
1 small onion, grated
1 carrot, peeled and grated
3 Tbsp cider vinegar
1 Tbsp brown sugar
2 eggs
½ cup all-purpose flour
½ tsp caraway seed
2 Tbsp fresh dill, chopped
½ tsp salt
Good grinding black pepper
Lard or shortening for frying

✦ In a large bowl mix together the flour, eggs, vinegar, brown sugar, caraway, dill, salt, and pepper until smooth. Add the onion, cabbage, apple, and carrot to the batter. Toss to combine. Let the mixture sit for 5 minutes and toss again.

Heat shortening or lard in a skillet over a medium flame. When the fat is hot but not smoking, drop heaping tablespoons of the mixture into a skillet. Fry 2–3 minutes on each side till browned and cooked through. Drain on absorbent paper and serve immediately.

Straw Potatoes

Yield 4 servings

These fried potatoes resemble a bed of straw laid down in a stall for livestock. They are especially compatible with grilled meats and fish.

4 good-size potatoes, peeled
4 Tbsp butter
2 Tbsp vegetable oil
Salt and freshly ground black pepper to taste

✦ Place the peeled potatoes in a bowl and cover with cold water until ready to cook so they won't discolor. The potatoes must be grated right before cooking to ensure cohesion. If the potatoes are grated and then held in water, they will become waterlogged and will produce a dense or heavy pancake. Water also rinses away the starch that gives potatoes the ability to stick together.

Melt 2 tablespoons of the butter with the oil in a large, heavy skillet over low heat. Meanwhile, grate the potatoes onto a towel and wring them dry. Once the butter has melted, increase the heat to high. When the butter and oil are bubbling, put the potatoes in the pan and pat them lightly into a pancake with a spatula. Cook over high heat for 3 minutes or until the underneath has a good, even coloring. Spread the remaining butter on top of the potatoes and then flip the pancake. Reduce the heat and cook for a further 5–8 minutes over medium heat. The pancake should be cooked through and nicely browned on the bottom. Slide the pancake onto absorbent paper and pat dry. Season to taste with salt and pepper. Cut into wedges and serve immediately.

Brussels Sprouts with Orange Butter
Yield 4 servings

Fresh Brussels sprouts bear little resemblance to those sour, soggy, orbs that reduce children to tears. Fresh sprouts are pleasant and tender and call for only simple embellishment. Gardeners know they are sweeter after a good hard frost or two. Harvest usually begins around Columbus Day.

When purchasing, look for firm, bright green Brussels sprouts without wilted leaves. Although the texture of wilted Brussels sprouts can be revived by soaking them in ice water, there is nothing you can do for the flavor except to mask it. Eat them when they are in season and remember how good they were until next year.

1 lb fresh Brussels sprouts
2 Tbsp butter
Juice 2 oranges
Juice 1 lemon
Salt and pepper to taste

✦ Peel the outer leaves from the sprouts and cut off the stems at their base. Cut the sprouts in half from top to bottom. This will decrease their cooking time and yield a sweeter vegetable. Bring a pot of water to a boil and then add the sprouts. Average-size sprouts take only 3 minutes to be crisply tender. Plunge them immediately into ice water to stop their cooking and to set the color. When cool, drain and reserve.

Squeeze the juice from the oranges and lemon into a skillet. Place over a medium flame and reduce until the consistency of maple syrup. Do not allow the juices to caramelize. Add the butter to the pan and swirl into the syrup. Add the Brussels sprouts and toss them with the orange butter until heated through and glazed. Add a spoonful of water to the pan if it starts to take on color. Pile the glazed sprouts into a bowl and serve immediately.

Maple-Baked Beans
Yield 8–10 servings

This traditional companion to baked ham, codfish cakes, and frankfurters never loses its popularity. Serve these mellow beans along with Steamed Brown Bread (see Chapter 8, Breads and Breakfast Cakes) and coleslaw (see this chapter, Coleslaw with Apples and Mustard).

1 lb (2 cups) beans (see method below)
2 qt water
1 cup maple syrup, preferably dark amber
1 cup sweet or hard cider
2 Tbsp cider vinegar
¼ tsp black pepper, freshly ground
2 tsp dry mustard
1 tsp ground ginger
1 tsp ground savory
½ cup onion, chopped fine
1 tsp salt
½ lb salt pork or slab bacon (about 1 inch thick)

✦ I prefer a small bean such as navy or pea when making this dish. Other popular legumes include Yellow Eye, Soldier, Cranberry, and Great Northern. Cranberry is perhaps the most traditional bean used in Vermont. All beans have different characteristics so keep an eye on them and be prepared for a slightly longer or shorter cooking time.

Cover the beans with the water and leave to soak at room temperature overnight; or you may quick-soak the beans by placing them in a pot with the water, cover, and boil for 2 minutes. Remove from the heat and leave covered for 1 hour. Whichever method you choose, drain the water from the beans and reserve it for their cooking.

Place the salt pork in a saucepan and cover with cold water. Bring to a boil, reduce the heat, and simmer uncovered for 10 minutes. Drain and score in a checkerboard pattern on the meat side without cutting through the rind.

Preheat oven to 275°F.

Place the dry ingredients in a bowl, add the vinegar, stir to a paste, and then stir in the cider. Combine the beans, maple syrup, onions, and spice mixture in a bean pot or a narrow, high-sided, covered casserole dish. Add 2 cups of the reserved bean water and stir together. Place the salt pork, cut side up, on top of the beans. Cover and place in a preheated 275°F oven.

The beans must cook very slowly, absorbing the liquid and seasonings. A long cooking time is essential so the beans will soften without falling apart. Check the beans occasionally, adding more of the reserved bean water if necessary. It is impossible to accurately determine the cooking time because of so many variables: the shape of the cooking vessel, type of bean used, and the heating characteristics of individual ovens, but 6–8 hours is a good rule of thumb, with the longer cooking time generally producing a superior result.

Once you have determined that the beans are done, remove them from the oven and allow them to rest at least ½ hour before serving. The perfect baked bean should be mealy but not mushy. There should be enough liquid to form a nice sauce. A spoonful of beans should flow slightly on a plate, not clump together or sit in a high, dry pile.

Roasted Chestnuts
Yield 4 servings

Available throughout the winter months, these meaty nuts are a delightful complement for game dishes, poultry, and pork. Hot roasted chestnuts are great after a day spent outside. Serve them with mugs of steaming mulled cider (see Chapter 1, section on Apples, Cider Apples).

Because of the chestnut blight, few native trees remain in the United States. Native chestnut trees have large spear-shaped, toothed leaves, and the nuts are covered by distinctive bristly husks. Each husk contains 2 or 3 nuts.

The inedible horsechestnut grows on a tree having palm-shaped leaves, grouped in 7–9 wedge-shaped leaflets. The nuts are contained in 3-part thorny husks. These nuts are poisonous and should not be eaten. Most chestnuts available in U.S. stores are grown in Europe.

1 lb chestnuts
1 tsp butter

✦ *Preheat oven to 425°F.*

Cut an X on the flat side of each chestnut with a sharp-pointed knife to avoid explosion and to facilitate peeling. Melt the butter in a heavy skillet over low heat. Add the chestnuts and roll them around until the shells are shiny. Place the skillet in a preheated 425° oven and roast for 15–20 minutes or until the chestnuts are tender when tested with a knife.

Chestnuts may also be roasted in a covered barbecue. Place the skillet of buttered chestnuts on the grill rack and put the lid on the grill. Leave the draft (on top) and the damper (on the bottom) open to maintain a hot temperature. Roast until tender, about 15–20 minutes. The chestnuts will absorb the smoky flavor of the charcoal like those hawked by street vendors in the city. Peel the chestnuts while they are warm, toss with sweet butter and salt, and serve warm.

Red Bliss Potatoes Baked with Spruce Boughs
Yield 4 servings

The dearth of fresh herbs during the winter months can be frustrating. These little potatoes absorb the evergreen essence. Uncover this dish at tableside to scent the room with the air of the forest. Serve with roasted venison, lamb, or feathered game (see Chapter 4, White Meats and Poultry, and Chapter 5, Red Meats and Duckling).

8 Red Bliss potatoes, no larger than a hen's egg
4 Tbsp butter
Good handful small spruce boughs
Salt and black pepper, freshly ground

✦ *Preheat oven to 325°F.*

Lay down a bed of the pine boughs in a covered casserole dish. Nest the potatoes in the boughs, season with salt and pepper, and dot each potato with the butter. Cover the dish and bake in a preheated 325° oven for 40 minutes or until the potatoes will yield easily when pierced with a fork. At this point they will be ·crisp-tender and subtly flavored. I like to leave them covered, in a warm place, for a further half hour so they will be waxy and deeply redolent of the spruce.

Preserves and Condiments

✦

Seedless Blackberry Apple Jam

Whole Strawberry Preserves

Spiced Apple Butter

Peach Preserves

Seedless Raspberry Jam

Wild Blueberry Preserves

Cranberry Apple Conserve

Sweet-and-Sour Onion Marmalade

Farmhouse Tomato Ketchup

Mayonnaise

Sharp Cheddar Cheese Salad Dressing

♦

Vinaigrette

Maple-Mustard Salad Dressing

Fresh Mint Sauce

Barbecue Sauce

Hot Pepper Relish

Preserved Sekel Pears

Pickled Chanterelles

Dilled Cucumber Relish

Double-Sour Tarragon Pickles

Dilled Green Tomatoes

Savory Green Beans

Storebought products cannot rival the flavor of homemade preserves, relishes, pickles, or salad dressings. The effort involved to make these delicacies is outweighed by the results. Not only are they the perfect addition to a meal, a brightly colored jar of preserves can serve as a thoughtful present or "hostess gift."

Putting up preserves and relishes is a satisfying method of extending the harvest. Whether you raise your own fruits and vegetables, buy them at market stands, or harvest them at a "pick-your-own" operation, you are rewarded with economy as well as homemade goodness.

Follow some basic rules to ensure success. Fruits and vegetables should be washed of insecticides and dirt and then drained before peeling, hulling, or slicing to avoid their absorption of superfluous water. Pick over the produce to eliminate bugs, leaves, and other natural debris.

Avoid the use of iron pots, for the acidity of fruits and of the vinegar used for pickling can react with the iron and adversely affect the flavor. Stir the bottom of the pot with a wooden spoon while cooking to prevent burning. Skim the foam from the surface as it accumulates. For every 550 feet of altitude above sea level, subtract 1° F from the jelly stage temperatures I have given.

It is paramount to observe proper canning procedures and can only products designed to be processed. Check jars for cracks or chips and discard them if they are not perfect. The jars must be perfectly clean, and *hot*, before being filled; my preference is to err on the side of safety and sterilize them at this point. Disk lids must be prepared (short preboil) according to the manufacturer's directions. When filling the jars, leave the stipulated headspace between the disk lids and the surface of the contents. Adjust the screwbands firmly to hold the lid in place; if they are tightened too much, air inside the jar cannot be vented to ensure a strong vacuum seal. Process the jars with a boiling water bath in a covered stockpot or similar deep kettle, with a rack to rest the jars on. The water should cover the lids by 1½–2 inches. Always process the jars for the full time given, beginning timing when the water returns to a boil. After the jars have cooled, check for a proper seal by pressing down on the lid; a secure lid is concave and will not spring back. Remove the bands from the jars during storage to prove that the seal is still good. Screw a band back onto a jar before giving it as a gift. Refrigerate jars after opening.

Seedless Blackberry Apple Jam
Yield 5–6 half-pints

Everyone loves the flavor of dark, luscious blackberries; but the seeds offend many. It is easy to remove them. This recipe combines a smooth puree of berries with soft, finely diced apples.

2 qt ripe blackberries
4 cups sugar
Juice 1 lemon
4 cups McIntosh apples, ¼-inch dice

✦ Pick over the berries to remove any debris and bugs. Blackberries don't need washing since they grow so high above the ground, unless they have been sprayed with insecticides or come from a dusty roadside. Mash the berries with the sugar and lemon juice. Put them in a large pot over low heat. Gradually increase the heat as more liquid forms. Allow the mixture to boil for 10 minutes, then pass the blackberries through the finest disc of a food mill. Work all the pulp through, eliminating only the seeds. Return the jam to the heat. Add the apple dice and cook until the mixture is thickened, skimming the foam from the surface as it accumulates.

Test for doneness with a spoon. Drops will ooze slowly and coalesce as they run off the spoon when the jam is ready. This proves to be a little before a thermometer registers jelly stage because of the pectin supplied by the apples. Ladle the hot jam into sterilized canning jars, leaving ¼-inch headspace. Process for 15 minutes, counting from the time the water returns to a boil.

Whole Strawberry Preserves
Yield 8–9 half-pints

Decreasing the cooking time of preserves helps to retain the just-picked taste. The day before you make this recipe, toss the berries with sugar; overnight the combination will create a syrup. Boil the syrup to jelly stage before adding the berries. The cooking time is halved, the garden-fresh flavor of the strawberries is captured, and the color of the preserves is improved.

4 qt ripe strawberries
8 cups sugar
Juice 1 lemon

✦ Wash the berries and drain well. When they are sufficiently dry, hull and cut in half only if they are huge. Toss the sugar, lemon juice, and strawberries together in a large bowl. Cover and leave overnight. Drain the liquid from the fruit into a large pot. Bring to a boil and cook until it reaches soft jelly stage (220°F). Add the berries and continue to boil until it reaches soft jelly stage again. Skim the foam from the surface.

Ladle the hot preserves into sterilized canning jars, leaving ¼-inch headspace. Process for 15 minutes, counting from when the water returns to a boil.

Spiced Apple Butter
Yield 8–9 half-pints

Enjoy this old-fashioned favorite on toast, hot split biscuits, popovers, or baked on salmon fillets and ham steaks.

The color of apple butter can vary dramatically, depending on the type of apple used—from the light golden hue of Peach apples to the barn red of crabapples to assorted siennas and umbers from McIntosh, Wealthy, Macoun, Lodi, or mongrel dooryard trees. Avoid iron pots, for iron will turn the butter black and give an off-flavor. Avoid powdered spices, too, for they discolor the butter and give it a bitter flavor. Sauce apples will make the best apple butter (see Chapter 1, Apple Chart: column: Use).

> 8 lb apples, crabapples, or a combination
> 2 cups sweet cider
> 2 cups cider vinegar
> 2 cups light brown sugar
> 1 cup maple syrup
> 2 sticks cinnamon
> 1 tsp whole cloves
> 1 tsp allspice berries
> 1 whole nutmeg

✦ Quarter the apples, but do not remove the cores or the peels. These are the main sources of natural pectin that sets the butter. Place the prepared apples in a heavy pot with the vinegar and cider, cover, and cook over low heat until softened. Pass through a food mill, using a fine disc, and return to the pot. Tie up the spices in a piece of cheesecloth or muslin and smash with a hammer to release their flavor. Add the spice bag to the applesauce with the maple syrup and brown sugar. Cook over low heat, uncovered, until reduced by about one-half. To test for doneness place a spoonful on a plate. It is ready when thick, jamlike, and no longer exuding liquid.

Discard the spice bag. Spoon the hot apple butter into clean, hot jars, leaving ¼-inch headspace. Process for 15 minutes, counting from the time the water returns to a boil.

Peach Preserves
Yield 6 half-pints

The subtle flavor and texture of peach preserves make them suitable for topping waffles and ice cream, sponge cake, cheesecake, or for lining a pie shell before adding buttermilk custard or raspberries.

5 lb ripe peaches
5 cups sugar
Juice and finely grated zest of 1 lemon

✦ Bring a large pot of water to a boil and plunge the peaches into it three or four at a time. The water should continue boiling when the fruit is added. Blanch the peaches for 15–20 seconds, remove with a slotted spoon, and immerse in ice water. Slip the skins from the peaches, cut them in half, and remove the stones. Slice the peaches, put in a bowl, and add the lemon juice and zest. Add the sugar and toss with the peaches.

Let the mixture sit for an hour or so, long enough for the sugar to melt and make a little syrup. This will decrease the chances of the peaches burning in the early stages of cooking. Peaches scorch easily so remember to watch them carefully. Pour the peach mixture into a pot, place on low heat, and increase the temperature as more liquid forms. Bring to a boil and stir occasionally to prevent the peach mixture from sticking to the bottom. Skim off the foam during cooking.

Cook until thick. Drops should ooze slowly and coalesce from a spoon when tested. This is slightly before jelly stage because of the thickening action of the peaches. There is no need to use a candy thermometer. Ladle the hot preserves into clean, hot jars, leaving ¼-inch headspace and process for 15 minutes, counting from the time the water returns to a boil.

Seedless Raspberry Jam
Yield 5 half-pints

Raspberries may be the most delicate of all fruits. They lend their flowery charm to salads, appetizers, main dishes, and desserts. Raspberry jam is wonderfully versatile; but who can resist it all by itself on a hot, buttered biscuit.

3 qt fresh raspberries
6 cups sugar

✦ Toss the sugar and raspberries together in a bowl. Cover and leave overnight. Pour the berries and liquid into a saucepan and bring to a boil. Reduce the heat and simmer for 10 minutes. Skim off the foam as it accumulates.

Pass the mixture through the finest disc of a food mill or work through a wire strainer into another saucepan. Press through the pulp; eliminate only the seeds. Return the pot to the heat and cook until a candy thermometer registers 220°F (soft jelly stage). Ladle the hot jam into sterilized canning jars, leaving ¼-inch headspace and process for 15 minutes, counting from the time the water returns to a boil.

Wild Blueberry Preserves
Yield 4–5 half-pints

In midsummer Vermont hillsides and shaded areas along old dirt roads and stone walls yield a bumper crop of low-bush blueberries. It takes a bit more picking to gather enough of these small wild berries for a pie or batch of jam; but the extra work is worth it. Their concentrated, spicy flavor is so unlike the supermarket variety, they seem like a totally different fruit.

2 qt ripe blueberries
4 cups sugar
Juice 1 orange and 1 lemon

✦ Pick over the berries to remove stems, leaves, and bugs. Wash and drain well. Place the blueberries in a bowl with the sugar and orange and lemon juice. Toss together and leave overnight. Drain the liquid from the berries into a large pot. Bring to a boil and cook until it reaches soft jelly stage (220°F). Add the berries, return to a boil, and cook until it again reaches soft jelly stage. Skim the foam from the surface as it cooks.

Ladle the hot preserves into sterilized canning jars, leaving ¼-inch headspace. Process for 15 minutes, counting from the time the water returns to a boil.

Cranberry Apple Conserve
Yield 4 half-pints

A conserve lies somewhere between a relish and a sauce. The American equivalent of chutney is usually made from several types of fruit and sometimes nutmeats. This tangy, colorful version is a fine companion for venison, turkey, duckling, goose, or suckling pig.

2 cups sugar
¼ cup water
1 cup cider vinegar
½ tsp black peppercorns, cracked
¼ tsp cloves, ground
2 tsp cinnamon, ground
Juice and finely grated zest of 1 orange
1 lb cranberries
1 cup sweet cider
3 large pie apples, peeled, cored, ½-inch dice
¼ cup brandy or applejack

✦ Put the sugar and water in a heavy pot that is not iron, which will give an off-color and off-taste to the acidic conserve. Cook over medium heat until golden brown. Add the vinegar and spices. Once the vinegar has scalded, add the cider and the orange juice and zest. Bring to a boil and add the cranberries. Cook until they burst and the mixture has noticeably thickened, about 5 minutes. Add the apples and cook until they have just softened, about 3 minutes. Remove from the heat and stir in the brandy.

This spicy conserve will keep for months in the refrigerator. It can also be put up in canning jars. Leave ¼-inch headspace and process for 15 minutes, counting from the time the water returns to a boil.

Sweet-and-Sour Onion Marmalade
Yield 4 half-pints

Serve this choice condiment with hot or cold smoked meats, pâtés, or roasted pork, turkey, or veal.

3 lb onions, peeled, ¼-inch dice
6 Tbsp vegetable oil
1 cup sugar
1 cup sweet cider
½ cup cider vinegar
½ tsp allspice, ground
½ tsp cloves, ground
½-inch piece fresh ginger, peeled and minced
4 cloves garlic, minced
2 Tbsp fresh parsley, chopped
4 Tbsp tomato paste
1 Tbsp pickling salt

✦ Heat the oil in a heavy pot over medium-high heat. Add the onions and cook until they are transparent, stirring occasionally. Add the sugar and cook until the liquid has evaporated and the onions are golden brown. Add the remaining ingredients, stir to combine, and reduce the heat to medium. Simmer for 20–30 minutes, until the mixture is like jam; adjust the seasoning to taste. Ladle the hot marmalade into clean, hot canning jars leaving ¼-inch headspace. Process for 10 minutes, counting from the time the water returns to a boil.

Farmhouse Tomato Ketchup
Yield 4 half-pints

This is how ketchup used to taste before the sweet commercial concoction became popular. It is a spicy, sweet, and sour condiment—marvelous with hamburgers and fried potatoes.

5 lb tomatoes, peeled, seeded, and coarsely chopped
2 Tbsp vegetable oil
1 head garlic, peeled and chopped
½ tsp red pepper, crushed
1 medium onion, peeled and diced
1 tsp mustard powder
½ tsp allspice berries
1 stick cinnamon
1 cup brown sugar
2 cups red wine vinegar
2 Tbsp pickling salt

✦ Heat the vegetable oil in a heavy pot over medium heat. Cook the onions and spices until the onions are transparent, stirring occasionally. Add the garlic and cook for 1 minute. Add the sugar, stir to combine, and pour in the vinegar. Reduce the mixture by one-half, about 20 minutes. Add the tomatoes and simmer over low heat for 1 hour.

Pass the mixture through a food mill using a fine disc. Return the ketchup to the pot and reduce until thickened. Put half the ketchup into a blender and run at high speed. Pour the blenderized ketchup back into the pot and stir together. By pureeing half the ketchup in the blender, the whole mixture will be emulsified. It will not separate; and since only half the ketchup was put in the blender, the sauce will retain some texture. Ladle the hot ketchup into clean, hot jars leaving ¼-inch headspace. Process for 10 minutes, counting from the time the water returns to a boil.

Mayonnaise
Yield 1½ cups

Mayonnaise may be the most popular and versatile cold sauce in the world. It is useful as a sandwich spread, the vehicle for chilled salads, and a topping for baked fish and poultry. Homemade mayonnaise has an incomparable sheen and flavor. While using raw eggs is generally discouraged by the U.S. Department of Agriculture and many food scientists, the acidity of the vinegar in mayonnaise in effect "cooks" the egg yolks and largely eliminates any danger from bacteria. (For further information, see Chapter 1, Eggs.)

  2 large egg yolks
  1 Tbsp Dijon mustard
  1 tsp salt
  1 cup vegetable oil
  2 Tbsp white vinegar or lemon juice

✦ Mayonnaise can be made using a bowl and a whisk or more easily in an electric mixer. Having all your ingredients at room temperature is the key to success.

Put the yolks, mustard, and salt in the bowl of the mixer. Run the machine at high speed until the yolks become pale yellow and have gained in volume. Pour the oil into the yolks slowly, in a thin, steady stream. As the yolks absorb the oil, the mayonnaise becomes progressively lighter in color and texture. If the sauce begins to separate, add a few drops of vinegar to balance the emulsion.

When all the oil is incorporated, finish with vinegar or lemon juice. The mayonnaise will keep refrigerated for a couple of weeks. You can vary the flavor by finishing it with lime juice or a flavored vinegar such as tarragon or raspberry. Vary the flavor by adding fresh herbs, garlic, curry powder, tomato paste, whole-grain mustard, horseradish, etc.

Sharp Cheddar Cheese Salad Dressing
Yield 4 cups

A creamy dressing that gives new life to winter salad greens and is useful for impromptu salads such as a summer potato salad with fresh raw peas and mustard greens or a tasty combination of smoked ham, asparagus, and pasta.

>One recipe homemade mayonnaise (1½ cups)
>1½ cups buttermilk
>1 lb sharp Cheddar cheese, grated (about 4 cups)
>1 Tbsp Dijon mustard
>⅛ tsp cayenne pepper, ground
>½ tsp Worcestershire sauce

✦ Combine mayonnaise, buttermilk, mustard, cayenne, and Worcestershire in a mixing bowl. Add the grated Cheddar and work with a fork until the mixture thickens. Cover and refrigerate overnight so the flavors can meld before using.

Vinaigrette
Yield one pint

A classic light dressing that highlights the fresh greens and vegetables of summer. Try it as a marinade for game and as a basting medium for spit-roasted or grilled meats and fish.

¾ cup vegetable oil
¾ cup olive oil
½ cup red wine vinegar
Juice 1 lemon
½ tsp salt
1 tsp black peppercorns, cracked
1 Tbsp shallots or onion, minced
1 tsp dried thyme leaves
1 clove garlic, minced

✦ Whisk together all the ingredients in a bowl at least 2 hours before using. This dressing is a temporary emulsion so it must be rewhisked before each use to redistribute the parts into the whole. It will keep indefinitely if refrigerated but should be brought to room temperature before using.

Maple-Mustard Salad Dressing
Yield one pint

This dressing combines some favorite Vermont flavors. Try it on spinach and bacon salad, on chilled pasta and vegetables, as a piquant dressing for cold roasts or as a marinade for game.

1½ cups vegetable oil
½ cup cider vinegar
⅓ cup maple syrup
Juice 1 lemon
1 Tbsp Dijon mustard
1 Tbsp whole-grain mustard
½ tsp rubbed (ground) sage
½ tsp black peppercorns, cracked
2 Tbsp fresh chives, chopped
½ tsp salt

✦ Whisk together all the ingredients in a bowl at least 2 hours before using. This dressing is a temporary emulsion so it must be rewhisked before each use to redistribute the parts into the whole. It will keep indefinitely if refrigerated but should be brought to room temperature before using.

Fresh Mint Sauce
Yield 3 cups

Mint grows just about anywhere it is wet. Explore along streams, ponds, drainage ditches in pastures, or a wet spot behind your home. Identify it by its square stems. If you don't happen to live in the country, mint is usually available in supermarkets. Cold mint sauce is almost always paired with lamb, but I suggest you try it with peas, game, and root vegetables.

1 cup cider vinegar
1 cup light brown sugar
1 cup water
1 Tbsp cornstarch
½ cup mint leaves, chopped fine

✦ Heat the vinegar, sugar, and half the water in a saucepan over medium heat. Bring to a boil and cook until the sugar has dissolved. Mix the remaining water with the cornstarch and pour into the boiling liquid. Stir until smooth and simmer for 1 minute. Add the mint leaves, bring just to a boil, and remove from the heat.

This sauce will keep indefinitely if refrigerated. The leaves settle to the bottom of the storage container, so it must be shaken or stirred before using. Allow the sauce to come to room temperature before serving.

Barbecue Sauce
Yield about 1 pint

Who can resist the smoky flavor of food cooked over white-hot charcoal? The spicy sauce caramelizes on the outside, all crispy and blackened, sealing in the juices until the first bite releases the essence of summer eating pleasure.

1 cup cider vinegar
4 cloves garlic
1 medium onion, chopped fine
⅔ cup maple syrup (dark amber)
¼ tsp cinnamon, ground
1 inch fresh ginger, peeled and minced
1 cup black coffee
1 Tbsp cornstarch
½ tsp salt

✦ Place the vinegar, garlic, onion, cinnamon, ginger, salt, and maple syrup in a saucepan. Cook over medium heat until reduced by one-half, about 10 minutes. Mix the coffee and the cornstarch in a small bowl until the cornstarch is dissolved. Slowly pour the coffee into the sauce, stirring all the while. Boil for 1 minute until the mixture is thickened and translucent. Use this sauce to baste chicken, pork, beef, lamb, or game.

Hot Pepper Relish
Yield 8 half-pints

Enjoy this fiery condiment on eggs, hamburgers, hot dogs, popcorn, in soup, stews, chili, or anywhere you would like to add a little zing. Cool its fire by reducing the amount of peppers or add to the heat by increasing them to your taste.

4 Tbsp vegetable oil
3 cups onions in ¼-inch dice
1–2 lb fresh cayenne or other hot peppers (such as jalapeño, super chili, or serrano chili)
2 Tbsp fresh parsley, chopped, or 1 Tbsp dried
2 Tbsp fresh basil, chopped, or 1 Tbsp dried
2 tsp dried leaf thyme
1 Tbsp dried oregano
1 tsp cumin seeds, toasted in a skillet until fragrant and crushed in a mortar
1 head garlic, minced
½ cup light brown sugar
1 qt good red wine vinegar
2 qt tomatoes, peeled, seeded, and in ½-inch dice
2 Tbsp pickling salt

✦ There is a lot of chopping, slicing, and mincing in making this relish. Plan on preparing all the vegetables before you begin the cooking.

Remove the crowns from the tomatoes and score an X through the skin on the opposite end to make peeling easier. Bring a large pot of water to a boil. Plunge the tomatoes, a few at a time, into it and blanch for 15 seconds. Remove with a slotted spoon and plunge them into ice water. Slip the skins from the tomatoes, cut them in half, remove the seeds, and cut them into ½-inch dice.

Cut the crowns from the peppers and discard. Slice crosswise into thin rings but do not remove the seeds. Some people suggest wearing rubber gloves when handling hot peppers. I have never felt the need although it is strongly recommended that you do not put your hands to your eyes or other sensitive parts of your anatomy while handling the peppers or soon afterward. Prepare the remaining items as directed in the list of ingredients.

Heat the oil in a heavy pot over medium heat. Cook the onions, peppers, herbs, and spices until the onions are transparent, stirring occasionally. Add the garlic and cook for 1 minute. Add the sugar, stir to combine, and pour in the vinegar. Cook the mixture until it is reduced by one-half, about 20 minutes. Add the tomatoes, stir together, and simmer over low heat until thickened, about 2 hours.

As the relish thickens, you should stir it from time to time to make sure it doesn't stick on the bottom and burn. The finished product should be the consistency of spaghetti sauce. Ladle the hot relish into clean, hot canning jars leaving ¼-inch headspace. Process for 15 minutes, counting from the time the water returns to a boil. Hot pepper relish improves if allowed to age in the jelly cupboard. Like a fine bottle of wine, it must be given the opportunity to ripen to its full glory.

Preserved Sekel Pears
Yield 3 pints

These little fruits are also known as sugar pears. No larger than a crabapple, their appearance always makes me think of holiday dinners. My mother preserved them in hugh batches and trotted them out on special occasions. Blushed pink by cranberry juice, they have a snappy taste that goes well with just about any roast.

3 lb Sekel pears, peeled
Whole cloves as needed
2½ cups cranberry juice
1 cup cider vinegar
1 cup sugar

✦ Peel the pears without removing the stems. Stick each pear with a clove. Bring the cranberry juice, vinegar, and sugar to a boil. Add the pears and cook for 2 minutes. Pack the fruit into clean, hot canning jars. Pour the hot liquid into the jars leaving ½-inch headspace. Process for 15 minutes, counting from the time the water returns to a boil.

Pickled Chanterelles
Yield 4 pints

Chanterelles have a ribbed trumpet shape, a sweet flavor, and an aroma like apricots. Consult a handbook or take along a knowledgeable friend on your first search. When gathering these delectable wild mushrooms, use a small sharp knife to cut them cleanly at the base. This makes them easier to clean and leaves the forest floor intact. Most important, this method prevents the formation of a cavity attractive to slugs, which can destroy the fungus-producing mother spore and the next crop. Serve pickled chanterelles with cold sliced game, pâtés, fried chicken, stewed rabbit, or on a relish tray.

3 lb chanterelles, cleaned and trimmed
1½ cups white vinegar
1½ cups water
½ cup light brown sugar
2 Tbsp pickling salt

Place in Each Jar

1 slice onion, separated into rings
1 clove garlic, peeled
1 spray fresh thyme
1 sprig fresh tarragon

✦ Bring the water, vinegar, brown sugar, and salt to a boil. Add the cleaned chanterelles and simmer for 5 minutes. Remove with a slotted spoon and divide evenly among 4 sterilized canning jars. Place the onion, garlic, and herbs into the jars. Pour the hot liquid into each jar leaving ¼-inch headspace. Process for 10 minutes, counting from the time the water returns to a boil.

Dilled Cucumber Relish
Yield 8–9 half-pints

Serve this classic relish with hot dogs, hamburgers, mixed with mayonnaise for fried fish, in picnic salads, or on a relish tray.

The Cure
12 cups cucumbers, ⅛-inch dice
2 cups onions, ⅛-inch dice
½ cup pickling salt

The Pickling Solution
¼ cup fresh dill, chopped fine
1 tsp crushed red pepper
1½ cups cider vinegar
1½ cups water
1½ Tbsp pickling salt

✦ Rinse the cucumbers under cold water and drain. Cut off the ends and slice in half lengthwise. Scoop out the seeds and pulp. Dice the cucumbers and onions. Place them in a colander and toss with salt to cure. Place the colander over a deep bowl in the refrigerator to drain overnight. You will be surprised how much juice the vegetables express.

The next day, squeeze the remaining liquid from the vegetables with your hands. Wash under cold running water for at least 5 minutes to be sure the residual salt has been rinsed away. Drain well and toss with the dill leaves and red pepper.

Bring the vinegar, water, cucumber mixture, and salt to a boil. Ladle into the canning jars leaving ¼-inch headspace. Make sure there are no air bubbles before you screw on the canning rings. Lower the canning rack into boiling water and process for 10 minutes, counting from when the water returns to a boil.

Double-Sour Tarragon Pickles
Yield 6 pints

A change of pace from the usual dill pickle, the pleasantly sour, herbal flavor contributes to the enjoyment of smoked meats, deli-style sandwiches, and pâtés.

4 lb small pickling cucumbers
4 cups white vinegar
2 cups water
4 Tbsp pickling salt

Place in Each Jar
2 sprays fresh tarragon
1 sprig fresh thyme
1 bay leaf
2 cloves garlic, peeled
½ tsp black peppercorns

✦ Choose firm, freshly picked cucumbers that are about the size of your thumb for a crisp little mouthful or two. Scrub them under cold running water and drain well. Pack the cucumbers into the canning jars. Place the herbs, garlic, and peppercorns into the sterilized jars.

Bring the vinegar, water, and salt to a boil. Pour into the jars leaving ¼-inch headspace. Process for 10 minutes, counting from when the water returns to a boil.

Dilled Green Tomatoes
Yield 7–8 pints

The killing frosts always come too soon for northern gardeners. When they roll down the mountainsides, leaving ghostly paths, it is time to bring the green tomatoes inside to ripen. Though many will turn red, the small, hard ones never come around and must be used as they are or be lost. Vermonters know this, ergo a wealth of green tomato recipes. Fried and served as a vegetable, baked with sugar in pies, made into chutney or relish or pickles are just a few of the possibilities. Green tomato pickles are a traditional accompaniment to a boiled dinner, or use them as you would a cucumber pickle.

> 5 lb small, hard green tomatoes, hulled and quartered
> 4 cups cider vinegar
> 4 cups water
> 4 Tbsp pickling salt

Place in Each Jar

> 2 cloves garlic, peeled
> Small handful of dill leaves, stems, or flowers, chopped
> 1 tsp mustard seed
> 1 bay leaf
> 1 slice onion, separated into rings
> 1 small cayenne pepper or ¼ tsp red pepper, crushed

✦ Choose small, hard green tomatoes, rinse them under cold water, and drain. Hull out the cores, quarter them, and pack into sterilized canning jars with the garlic, herbs, onion, and spices. Arrange the dill and onions so that the jars will look attractive after they are processed. Bring the vinegar, water, and salt to a boil. Pour the hot liquid into the jars leaving ¼-inch headspace. Process the jars for 15 minutes, counting from the time the water returns to a boil.

Savory Green Beans
Yield 4 pints

Peppery and mintlike, savory is often called the "bean herb." Its small shiny leaves and lavender blossoms make it a beautiful addition to your herb garden. Try these crisp pickled beans in a tossed salad or include them on a relish tray.

2 lb green beans
2 cups white vinegar
2 cups water
1 cup sugar
2 Tbsp pickling salt

Place in Each Jar

2 large sprays summer savory
2 cloves garlic, peeled
1 slice onion, separated into rings

✦ Select tender medium-sized beans that will snap when bent. Wash the beans under cold water and trim the ends. Pack them into sterilized jars with the savory, garlic, and onion. Arrange the flavoring elements so that the jars will look attractive after processing.

Bring the vinegar, water, sugar, and salt to a boil. Pour the hot liquid into the jars leaving ¼-inch headspace. Process for 10 minutes, counting from the time the water returns to a boil. Sometimes the beans will pucker after canning. If this happens, don't worry—they will plump back up after a couple of weeks.

Breads and Breakfast Cakes

◆

Country White Bread

Whole Wheat Cheddar Bread

Honey Rice Bread

Buttermilk Rye Bread

Steamed Brown Bread

Vermont Johnnycake

Whole Wheat-Cornmeal Pancakes

Buttermilk Biscuits

Mount Mansfield Popovers

Cheddar Cheese and Chive Breadsticks

Crunchy Doughnuts

About Bread

Like so many basics, homemade bread has almost vanished from our culture. You won't find a recipe for bread in century-old cookbooks, for making bread was a task taken completely for granted. The mystique that surrounds the process is undeserved. There are few things so easily done, and fewer still that satisfy like making bread.

The initial steps offer a tactile and therapeutic activity that requires no more than 15 or 20 minutes—just enough to free your mind from the workaday world.

Bread requires only 4 ingredients—flour, yeast, water, and salt. One of the most beloved breads in the Western world, French bread, is based on these 4 components. Other ingredients are added to alter the texture, structure, flavor, or storage qualities of the loaf; for example, for seeded rye bread, substitute rye flour for a portion of the white flour and toss in some seeds. After a while you will find there is no need to follow recipes. You will be able to make whatever kind of bread you wish merely by adding ingredients to produce the desired result. Knowing what part each plays in making up the loaf will guide your judgment.

Flour is the foremost ingredient. I recommend an unbleached, unbromated flour made from winter wheat. It should be creamy in color, and it should clump together when squeezed in your hand. Only wheat flour has the necessary building blocks of gluten that enable the dough to rise and hold its shape. Always sift your flour, even if the bag claims it is "presifted." Lumps are likely to form during packing and shipping.

The next important ingredient is yeast, a single-celled plant that converts starch into sugar for its food, expelling carbon dioxide and alcohol. Yeast thrives in warm, moist environments such as bread dough. It is available fresh in cake form or dried in individual packets or jars. Both types perform with equal vigor. To revive the yeast, mix it in a small ceramic or stainless steel bowl with a splash of warm water and some flour. Place this thin paste in a warm spot for a few minutes. When small bubbles appear, it is ready to use. Do not add sugar directly to the yeast, for direct contact with sugar can reduce its life. Too much yeast will affect the flavor of the bread shorten its shelf life, and produce an overblown, dry loaf. Too little yeast is not really possible, only a longer rising time will result.

You can control rising times by the amount of yeast you add to the dough. If you plan to mix the bread in the morning before work and bake it in the evening, cut down on the amount you add and let it rise in a cool place. Generally speaking, the dough should be placed in a warm, draftless place to rise. In the summertime anywhere in the room will suffice as a warm place. A temperature around 90°F, but no warmer, is desirable unless you want the rising to take longer. Dough always rises more rapidly on a hot, humid day than on a cold one. There is no reason to worry if the dough quadruples in volume or grows out of the bowl. It is doing what it needs to do. Simply punch it down and make your loaves when you are ready. A long rising gives the dough the time it needs to develop the rich, nutty flavor that only extended ripening can produce. This flavor is not found in storebought bread.

Any pure water works. Only heavily chlorinated waters affect the bread's flavor. Other liquids can be substituted for water. Milk prolongs shelf life and softens the crust, desirable for rolls and buns. The temperature of the liquid should never exceed 120°F. Anything above will kill the yeasts and affect the starch in the flour.

Salt is necessary to retard the action of the yeast, for the development of a good crust, and for seasoning. Any pure, untreated variety will do. Too much salt injures the yeast or makes the bread unpalatable; too little yields a very strange and tasteless loaf.

Basic Method

Have all your ingredients at hand. A large ceramic or stainless steel bowl is best for mixing and rising. Plastic has no thermal conductivity and therefore does not help the dough to rise.

Mix the yeast in a small bowl with a little flour and warm water and leave it to reactivate while measuring the remaining ingredients. I have a standard flour sifter that holds 6 cups of flour. To make a recipe requiring 12 cups of white flour, I simply place the sifter into the center of my work bowl and dump the flour into it, filling it up twice. Each sifterful requires 1 tablespoon of salt, which I add each time I fill it. After sifting, stir the flour to distribute the salt evenly. When a recipe calls for 8 cups of white flour and 4 cups of whole wheat, estimate that amount in the sifter. Fill it up all the way once with white flour. The second time fill it two-thirds full with whole wheat and the rest white.

Make a well in the center of the flour, then add the yeast mixture and warm water all at once. Mix it into a dough and knead it in the bowl. Turn the dough over and over on itself for about 5 minutes. If it is too soft and sticky, work more flour into it. If it is too dry and has not become a smooth resilient mass, add a little more water. Pour a tablespoon of vegetable oil onto the dough and rub it all over to prevent sticking as it rises. Cover the bowl with plastic wrap, a lid, or a damp towel. Place in a warm, draftless place and go about your business. Wait until the dough has at least doubled in volume. This can be a couple of hours in the summer or half a day during the colder months. Again, timing is not crucial. When the dough is ready, punch it down and turn it onto a lightly floured counter. Cut into equal pieces with a sharp knife. Shape the loaves as you choose. They do not have to be baked in loaf tins unless you are using a very soft dough that needs containment. Form the dough into round or oblong loaves. Place, with the folded side down, in pans that have been greased and dusted with flour. I like to use pie tins for round loaves. Dust the tops lightly with flour.

Preheat oven to 410°F.

Cover the prepared loaves and allow them to rise in a warm place until doubled in volume. With a razor blade or a sharp knife, slash the tops ½ inch deep, the length of the loaf. This allows controlled expansion of the loaves and prevents them from separating along the bottom edge during baking. Preheat the oven and allow the loaves to rise, uncovered, until the oven is up to temperature.

Bake on the center shelf of a preheated 410° oven for 40 minutes. Test for doneness by tapping the loaves on the bottom. A practiced ear will distinguish the hollow thump of a finished loaf from the dull thud of an undercooked one. Turn out onto a wire rack. When completely cool, seal the extra loaves in plastic bags and freeze. Pull a frozen loaf out of your freezer several hours before using.

After you have made a few loaves of bread, you'll observe the different properties of flours. Whole wheat produces a dense, somewhat drier dough. Rye flour always makes a softer and stickier dough. Don't try to correct these traits, which are characteristic of the grains. By measuring in the sifter and kneading in the bowl there is little to clean up. A recipe calling for 12 cups of flour makes 3 loaves of bread.

Country White Bread
Yield 3 loaves

A good all-purpose loaf with a chewy crust and a close texture. It is ideal for sandwiches, toast, or as a table loaf.

12 cups unbleached all-purpose flour
2 Tbsp salt
4½ cups water

Ingredients for Yeast Mixture
2 packages dried yeast (1 package during very warm weather)
1 Tbsp flour
¼ cup warm water

✦ In a small bowl make a thin paste with the yeast, 1 tablespoon flour, and ¼ cup warm water. Leave in a warm place to reactivate the yeast while you measure your ingredients.

Sift the flour with the salt into a bread-mixing bowl. Make a well in the center of the flour and pour in the water and yeast mixture. Work into a slightly sticky dough of medium consistency. Knead for 5 minutes, cover, and place in a warm, draftless place to rise. When it has tripled in volume, punch it down, and turn it onto a counter lightly dusted with flour.

Preheat oven to 410°F.

Cut the dough into 3 equal pieces with a sharp knife. Form into loaves and place in greased and floured pans. Use pie tins for round loaves and 2-quart loaf pans for rectangular ones. Sprinkle the loaves with a little flour, cover, and leave in a warm place until doubled in size. Uncover and slash the loaves with a razor blade or sharp knife, cutting ½ inch deep the length of the loaf. Two or three diagonal slashes or a crisscross also work well.

When the oven has come up to 410°, place the loaves on the center shelf and bake for 40 minutes. Test for doneness by tapping the bottoms of the loaves and listening for a hollow thump. Turn the bread from the pans onto a wire rack to cool. Cool to room temperature before slicing.

Whole Wheat Cheddar Bread

Yield 3 loaves

The nutlike flavor of stone-ground whole wheat and the tang of sharp Vermont Cheddar cheese combine well in this hearty bread. The cheese keeps the bread moist for several days. Especially good toasted and served with hearty soups and stews.

8 cups unbleached all-purpose flour
4 cups whole wheat flour (preferably stone ground)
2 Tbsp salt
4 cups water
2 cups (½ lb) grated sharp Cheddar cheese

Ingredients for Yeast Mixture

2 packages dried yeast (1 package during very warm weather)
1 Tbsp flour
¼ cup warm water

✦ In a small bowl make a thin paste with the yeast, 1 tablespoon of flour, and ¼ cup of warm water. Leave in a warm place to reactivate the yeast while you measure your ingredients.

Sift the white flour with the salt into a bread-mixing bowl and stir in the whole wheat flour. Rub the grated cheese into the flour and make a well in the center of the flour mixture. Pour in the water and yeast and work into a rubbery dough of a medium consistency. It should feel smooth and slightly sticky. Knead for 5 minutes, cover, and place in a warm, draftless place to rise. When it has tripled in volume, punch down and turn onto a counter lightly dusted with flour.

Preheat oven to 410°F.

Cut the dough into 3 equal pieces with a sharp knife. Form into loaves and place in greased and floured pans. Use pie tins for round loaves and 2-quart loaf pans for rectangular ones. Sprinkle the loaves with a little flour, cover, and leave in a warm place until doubled in size. Uncover and slash the loaves with a razor blade or sharp knife, cutting ½ inch deep the length of the loaf. Two or three diagonal slashes or a crisscross also work well.

Set the oven to 410°F. When it has come up to temperature, place the loaves on the center shelf and bake for 40 minutes. Test for doneness by tapping the bottoms of the loaves and listening for a hollow thump. Turn the bread from the pans onto a wire rack to cool. Cool to room temperature before slicing.

Honey Rice Bread
Yield 3 loaves

Rice and honey combine to produce a loaf that is moist without being doughy. This full-flavored bread has a medium-soft texture and a soft crust. It is very good for grilled sandwiches, French toast, and picnic or luncheon sandwiches that must stay fresh for hours.

1 cup short-grained rice (see method below)
2½ cups water
6 cups unbleached all-purpose flour
3 cups stone-ground whole wheat flour
2 Tbsp salt
⅔ cup clover honey
1½ cups milk

Ingredients for Yeast Mixture
2 packages dried yeast (1 package during very warm weather)
1 Tbsp flour
¼ cup warm water

✦ Short-grained rice becomes soft and starchy when cooked with an excess of water and will be easily assimilated in the bread. Most other types of rice will not meld as well with the dough and can become hard and unpalatable in the crust.

Bring the water to a boil, add the rice, and cook covered over low heat until all the water has been absorbed, about 45 minutes. Remove from the heat and leave covered for 5 more minutes. In a small bowl make a thin paste with the yeast, 1 tablespoon flour, and ¼ cup warm water. Leave in a warm place to reactivate the yeast while you measure your ingredients.

Sift the white flour with the salt into a bread-mixing bowl and stir in the whole wheat flour. Rub the warm rice into the flour until evenly distributed. Make a well in the center of the flour mixture and pour in the yeast paste, honey, and milk. Work into a slightly sticky dough of a medium consistency. Knead for 5 minutes, cover, and place in a warm, draftless place to rise. When it has tripled in volume, punch it down and turn it onto a counter lightly dusted with flour.

Preheat oven to 410°F.

Cut the dough into 3 equal pieces with a sharp knife. Form into loaves and place in greased and floured pans. Use pie tins for round loaves and 2-quart loaf pans for rectangular ones. Sprinkle the loaves with a little flour, cover, and leave in a warm place until doubled in size. Uncover and slash the loaves with a razor blade or sharp knife, cutting ½ inch deep the length of the loaf. Two or three diagonal slashes or a crisscross also work well.

When the oven has come up to 410°, place the loaves on the center shelf and bake for 40 minutes. Test for doneness by tapping the bottoms of the loaves and listening for a hollow thump. Turn the bread from the pans onto a wire rack to cool. Cool to room temperature before slicing.

Buttermilk Rye Bread

Yield 3 loaves

Buttermilk gives this loaf a subtle tang, similar to sourdough, and an even texture. This seeded, light rye bread has a medium-soft crust and a close texture, and it will slice as thin as you like.

> **8 cups unbleached all-purpose flour**
> **4 cups rye flour (preferably stone ground)**
> **2 Tbsp salt**
> **2 Tbsp caraway seeds**
> **1 Tbsp dill seeds**
> **1 Tbsp coriander seeds**
> **2 cups churned buttermilk (labeled *churned* on the product)**
> **2 cups water**

Ingredients for Yeast Mixture

> **2 packages dried yeast (1 package during very warm weather)**
> **1 Tbsp flour**
> **¼ cup warm water**

✦ In a small bowl make a thin paste with the yeast, 1 tablespoon flour, and ¼ cup warm water. Leave in a warm place to reactivate the yeast while you measure your ingredients.

Sift the white flour and salt into a bread-mixing bowl and stir in the rye flour. Bruise the caraway, dill, and coriander seeds in a mortar to release their flavor and stir into the flour mixture. Make a well in the center of the flour and pour in the buttermilk, water, and yeast mixture. Work into a slightly sticky dough of medium consistency. Knead for 5 minutes, cover, and place in a warm, draftless place to rise. When it has tripled in volume, punch it down and turn it onto a counter dusted with flour.

Preheat oven to 410°F.

Cut the dough into 3 equal pieces with a sharp knife. Form into loaves and place in greased and floured pans. Use pie tins for round loaves and 2-quart loaf pans for rectangular ones. Sprinkle the loaves with a little flour, cover, and leave in a warm place until doubled in size. Uncover and slash the loaves with a razor blade or sharp knife, cutting ½ inch deep the length of the loaf. Two or three diagonal slashes or a crisscross also work well.

When the oven has come up to 410°, place the loaves on the center shelf and bake for 40 minutes. Test for doneness by tapping the bottoms of the loaves and listening for a hollow thump. Turn the bread from the pans onto a wire rack to cool. Cool to room temperature before slicing.

Steamed Brown Bread
Yield 2 loaves

Rich, dark, and wholesome, this sweet bread is the traditional companion for baked beans, ham, and codfish cakes. Although it is made like a steamed pudding, it turns out rather like an old-world pumpernickel bread in texture but very American in flavor.

> **1 cup stone-ground cornmeal**
> **1 cup stone-ground rye flour**
> **1 cup stone-ground whole wheat flour**
> **1 tsp salt**
> **1 tsp baking soda**
> **2 cups buttermilk**
> **1 cup molasses**
> **1 cup raisins**   *(Continued)*

✦ Stir together the cornmeal, rye flour, whole wheat flour, and salt in a mixing bowl. Dissolve the baking soda in the buttermilk. Add the buttermilk and molasses to the flour mixture and work into a smooth batter. Fold in the raisins.

Butter two 1-quart pudding molds, or two 1-pound coffee cans, and pour in the batter. The molds should be no more than two-thirds full so that the batter can rise during the cooking. Cover the molds, or cans, with a double layer of aluminum foil, leaving a bit of headroom, and secure it with a piece of string.

Place the cans in a pot and fill with water so that the water comes one-third of the way up the cans. Cover the kettle and steam for 3 hours, checking the water level occasionally. To remove the finished bread from coffee cans, invert the can, open the bottom with a can opener, and push the bread through. Serve warm.

Vermont Johnnycake
Yield 8 servings

The name "johnnycake" is said to derive from small cornmeal cakes packed to provide sustenance on a journey. Thus journeycake became easily modified to johnnycake. The name survives in Vermont for a quickbread made from rich yellow cornmeal.

Early stone-ground cornmeal was softer and more flourlike than is the contemporary bland, highly processed version. Today stone-ground cornmeal can be found in natural food stores and on the shelves of some supermarkets. This johnnycake is golden brown in color, light in texture, and won't crumble when spread with sweet creamery butter.

1 cup stone-ground cornmeal
1 cup all-purpose flour
2 tsp baking powder
1 tsp salt
2–4 Tbsp maple syrup or 1–2 Tbsp molasses
1 cup milk
4 Tbsp butter
1 egg, beaten

✦ *Preheat oven to 425°F.*

Into a mixing bowl sift together the flour, baking powder, and salt. Warm the milk with the maple syrup and butter until the butter has melted. Add the beaten egg and the milk mixture to the cornmeal and work quickly into a batter. Pour into a greased and floured 8–9-inch cake tin. Bake on the center shelf of a preheated 425° oven 20–22 minutes. The johnnycake is puffed and golden when done. Let it rest for a few minutes before slicing. Cut into wedges and serve warm with butter to accompany soups, stews, chili, baked ham, roasted poultry, or for breakfast.

Whole Wheat-Cornmeal Pancakes
Yield 18 4-inch pancakes

Serve griddlecakes for breakfast, nooning, or as a side dish at the evening meal. These are nutritious and substantial, yet surprisingly light and soft.

   1 cup stone-ground cornmeal
   1 tsp salt
   2 Tbsp maple or brown sugar
   1 cup boiling water
   1 cup milk
   1 egg, beaten
   1 cup stone-ground whole wheat flour
   2 tsp baking powder
   2 Tbsp butter, melted

✦ Stir together in a ceramic or stainless steel mixing bowl the cornmeal, salt, and sugar. Stir the boiling water into the mixture and let rest for 5 minutes. Meanwhile stir together the flour and baking powder. Quickly stir the cornmeal, milk, and melted butter into the cornmeal.

Heat a griddle over a moderate flame and shine it with a pat of butter. Only a slight amount of fat is required to prevent the pancakes from sticking. The pancakes should not be fried. Cook until golden brown on the bottom and bubbles have formed on the top. Turn and cook for a further minute or two. Serve at once with butter, warm maple syrup, honey, or fruit preserves.

Buttermilk Biscuits
Yield 10–12 biscuits

The key to light, airy biscuits is a soft flour. The addition of cake flour reduces the batter's ability to form toughening glutens. The biscuits are free to aspire to great heights. Serve them directly from the oven for breakfast with honey and jam or at dinner with sweet butter or gravy.

2 cups unbleached all-purpose flour
1 cup cake flour
4 tsp baking powder
½ tsp baking soda
1 tsp salt
3 Tbsp chilled butter
1¼ cups buttermilk

✦ Sift together into a mixing bowl the flours, baking powder, baking soda, and the salt. Stir them together to ensure an even distribution of ingredients. Cut the butter into the flour, using a pastry cutter or a fork, until the mixture resembles cornmeal. Pour in the buttermilk and work quickly, with a fork, into a soft, sticky dough.
Preheat oven to 425°F.
Wash and dry your hands and coat them with flour. Snatch egg-sized lumps of the dough and tenderly form them into misshapen balls, flattening them slightly. Place the biscuits onto a greased and floured sheet pan, or pie tin, with the biscuits barely touching one another. They will grow together as they bake, thereby preventing the formation of side crusts, producing a more tender biscuit.
Bake on the center shelf of a preheated 425° oven for 15 minutes. The biscuits will be puffed and golden brown when they are done. Serve directly from the oven.

Mount Mansfield Popovers
Yield 8 large popovers

Named for their resemblance to the tallest mountain in Vermont, these popovers are a homey form of quickbread. Follow a few guidelines and you will make mountainous popovers, crispy and golden, filled with wispy fluff.

The batter should be smooth, free of lumps, and the consistency of chilled buttermilk. Let the batter rest, at room temperature, for 3 hours or simply strain it through a wire strainer. Mixing should be done by hand. Do not use a food processor or a blender, for these appliances produce too thick a batter that become more a pudding then a popover.

Use a flavorful fat such as roast beef or bacon drippings or butter. These drippings end up in the center of each popover and greatly enhance its flavor. Do not vary the heat. A straightforward oven temperature produces a very satisfactory result. It is important to warm the pan in the oven for a couple of minutes before you spoon in the batter.

Serve popovers directly from the oven with butter, apple butter, or jam. Popovers are also delicious at brunch filled with creamy scrambled eggs mixed with savory additions or for luncheon filled with creamed chicken, salmon, or wild mushrooms with fresh herbs.

1 cup unbleached all-purpose flour
1 tsp salt
1 cup milk
2 eggs, beaten
Good grating nutmeg
2 Tbsp sherry
5 Tbsp roast beef or bacon drippings or melted butter

◆ *Preheat oven to 375°F.*

Sift together into a mixing bowl the flour, salt, and nutmeg. Add the milk, sherry, and beaten eggs and mix quickly to a smooth batter. Stir in 1 tablespoon of the drippings or melted butter. Cover the batter and leave at room temperature for 3 hours, or simply strain it through a wire strainer to free it of lumps.

Prepare muffin or popover tins by pouring roughly 1½ tablespoons of drippings into each. Make sure that the sides of the cups are greased. Place the tins into the oven for a couple of minutes. They do not have to be smoking hot, but you should not start with a pan still cold from the pantry. Fill the tins two-thirds full with the batter. Bake on the lower shelf of a preheated 375° oven for 35–40 minutes. They are done when well puffed, richly brown, and the centers set.

Cheddar Cheese and Chive Breadsticks
Yield 2 dozen 6-inch sticks

Crisp and cheesy, these little sticks are perfect with soups, stews, or hors d'oeuvres such as melon and proscuitto, chicken wings, or crudités.

2½ cups unbleached all-purpose flour
½ cup whole wheat flour
¼ cup vegetable oil
¾ cup beer or ale
1 tsp salt
1 cup sharp Cheddar cheese, grated
2 Tbsp fresh chives, chopped
1 tsp Dijon mustard
Few drops Tabasco

Ingredients for Yeast Mixture
1 package dried yeast
1 Tbsp flour
¼ cup warm water

✦ In a small bowl make a thin paste with the yeast, 1 tablespoon flour, and ¼ cup warm water. Leave it in a warm place to start the yeast while you measure your ingredients.

Sift the flours and salt into a bread-mixing bowl and rub in the cheese. Add the beer, vegetable oil, chives, mustard, Tabasco, and the yeast mixture. Combine and knead for 5–10 minutes. The cheese should be completely incorporated into the dough. Cover and place in a warm, draftless place to rise. When the dough has tripled in volume, punch it down and turn it onto a counter lightly dusted with flour.

Preheat oven to 350°F.

Roll into a sausage shape and slice into 24 equal pieces. This is easiest to do by dividing it in half. Then divide each half and proceed from there. Roll each piece into a stick about 6 inches long. If the dough seems stiff or elastic, cover, and allow it to rest for 15 minutes. Place the sticks on a greased and floured baking sheet allowing room for them to expand without touching. Cover and allow to rise until doubled in volume. Brush lightly with beaten egg and sprinkle with a little coarse salt if desired. Make diagonal "French bread" slashes in the breadsticks with a razor blade. Bake in a preheated 350° oven 35–40 minutes or until nicely browned.

Recrisp the breadsticks in a 350° oven for 3–5 minutes before serving.

Crunchy Doughnuts
Yield 2 dozen doughnuts

These doughnuts adapt to any occasion. Crunchy on the outside and fragrant with spices, they are perfect for dunking in coffee or to accompany the time-honored spring tradition of sugar on snow—maple syrup boiled to thread stage (225–232°F on a candy thermometer) and drizzled over snow to make a rich caramel candy.

2½ cups unbleached all-purpose flour
1 cup cake flour
4 tsp baking powder
½ tsp salt
½ tsp nutmeg, freshly grated
Good pinch mace
1 cup granulated sugar
1 cup milk
2 eggs, beaten
3 Tbsp lard, shortening, or melted butter

✦ Sift together into a mixing bowl the flours, baking powder, salt, and spices. Stir in the sugar and add the milk, beaten eggs, and melted butter. Stir quickly into a sticky dough, cover, and refrigerate for 1 hour. This makes the dough more manageable and gives the gluten a chance to relax.

Roll out the dough on a lightly floured board to a thickness of ½ inch. Cut out rings with a floured doughnut cutter, using a straight downward push. Do not twist the cutter; this motion has the tendency to crimp the edges, which inhibits the rising potential of the dough.

Leave the cut doughnuts and doughnut holes to rest, uncovered, for 15 minutes. Meanwhile, heat about 2 inches of fresh shortening or lard in a heavy pot. Try to maintain a moderate temperature of 360° during the cooking. Fry the doughnuts, three or four at a time, for 1–2 minutes on each side. They are done when puffed and golden brown. Drain on absorbent paper.

Serve the doughnuts warm or at room temperature. Once the doughnuts have cooled, they can be dusted with powdered sugar, cinnamon sugar, dipped in melted chocolate, or glazed with a favorite icing. They are at their best served, just as they are, with steaming mugs of rich, black coffee.

Desserts

✦

Lemon Meringue Pie

Elmore Mountain Apple Pie

Cheese and Buttermilk Pie

Deep Dish Pumpkin Pie

Peach Pie

Strawberry Rhubarb Pie with Crumb Topping

Blueberry Pie

Cherry and Almond Tart

Chocolate Cake with Raspberry Buttercream

Spiced Apple Cake with Maple Frosting

Strawberry Shortcake

Creamy Rice Pudding

Indian Pudding Soufflé

Butternut Cookies

Could there be a more fitting conclusion to a meal than a freshly prepared homemade dessert? Time and love go into the preparation of these old-fashioned treats that have been enjoyed for generations by kids and grandparents alike.

The act of creation enhances the final experience of eating: peeling and slicing crisp-skinned apples, rolling out pastry, and carefully measuring spices and sugar give pleasure and a feeling of accomplishment. The warmth and aromas of baking fill the house, stimulating all the senses. There is magic to the chemistry that makes cakes rise and puddings set. A beautifully prepared dessert can stand as a piece of art, gratifying to have made and exquisite to behold. Desserts are a meal's grand finale. The last course eaten, the first remembered, they rank among the most vivid of sensual memories.

Flaky Pastry for Pies

The ideal pie crust is flaky, tender, and flavorful—firm enough to support the filling, tender enough to melt in your mouth. A balanced formula is important, but your technique is more important. For the best results, be sure to read through the instructions before you begin.

For a custard-type pie—pumpkin, for example—a closer grained, mealy crust to resist the liquid filling is best. Cut the fat into the flour until it is the consistency of cornmeal. A food processor will do this magnificently in a matter of seconds.

The choice of fat or combination of fats will alter the texture as well as the flavor of the pastry. Butter gives a wonderful flavor but contains 20 percent water. A provision for this water must be applied to your formula. Lard gives the flakiest result and vegetable shortening the most tender. I prefer to use a combination of butter and either lard or vegetable shortening to gain the advantages of both.

Sugar has a softening effect on the protein (gluten) in flour, but only if it dissolves before it is baked. Confectioner's sugar dissolves in the presence of the minute amount of liquid used in the basic recipe and improves the quality of the crust.

Water needs to be as cold as possible to prevent the fats from melting. Add it all at once and quickly massage the mixture together without overworking it.

Single 9–10-inch pie crust

1½ cups unbleached all-purpose flour
1 Tbsp confectioner's sugar
½ tsp salt
4 Tbsp unsalted butter, chilled
4 Tbsp lard or shortening, chilled
3 Tbsp ice cold water

Double or Lattice-Topped Pie Crust

3 cups unbleached all-purpose flour
2 Tbsp confectioner's sugar
1 tsp salt
8 Tbsp (¼ lb) unsalted butter, chilled
8 Tbsp lard or shortening, chilled
⅓ cup ice cold water

✦ Sift together the dry ingredients and stir them to distribute them evenly. Have the fats well chilled and cut into small pieces to expedite their incorporation into the flour. The object is to coat the particles of flour with the fat, thereby insulating them from the toughening effects of the water. Cut the fat into the flour with a pastry cutter or a fork until the mixture includes lumps of flour and fat the size of peas. The process must be accomplished before the fats have a chance to soften. Professional pastry chefs use their hands for this task. Move quickly and use only the fingertips, the coolest part of the hands. Gather the pastry into a ball and flatten it slightly. Wrap it in plastic wrap and refrigerate for at least 1 hour. This will relax the pastry and make it more manageable.

Preheat oven to 400°F.

Roll out the chilled pastry on a lightly floured board using a rolling pin that has been dusted with flour. If you are making a double-crust pie, divide the pastry in two and keep the other piece wrapped and refrigerated until required. Roll to an even thickness around ⅛ inch, without stretching the pastry. Wrap the pastry around the rolling pin and simply unroll it into the pie tin.

For single-crust pie, trim the pastry a good ½ inch beyond the rim of the tin. Dampen around the perimeter and fold it inward. Work up into a collar that stands above the rim, and flute the edge. Do this either by pinching or by pushing a knuckle into the outside of the pastry collar against two fingers on the inside. Prick the pastry with a fork, in a dozen or so places, to prevent steam trapped beneath the crust from creating bubbles. Place the pie shell in the freezer if you are not going to fill it immediately.

For a two-crust pie roll the pastry in the same manner, leaving a ½-inch overhang. Dampen the edge and place the top crust on the filled pie. Flute the edge, making sure the pie is sealed so you do not end up with a mess in your oven. Cut several small gashes in the top crust to allow steam to escape during baking.

To achieve a crisp bottom crust, first paint the inside of the pie shell with egg white or melted jam to insulate it from the juicy filling. Prick the bottom of the crust after painting, otherwise you are merely resealing the holes with the jam or egg white. Bake the pie on the bottom shelf of a preheated 400° oven. The heat will pass up through the pie rather than bearing down on it equally from all sides.

Lemon Meringue Pie

Fluffy, sweet meringue offsets the snappy tang of the lemon curd filling. This dessert is a perfect ending for a dinner of spicy pasta or fish.

Pastry for a single-crust pie

Lemon Filling

1 cup freshly squeezed lemon juice (4–5 lemons)
1 cup sugar
1 Tbsp lemon zest, grated fine
4 egg yolks; reserve the whites for the meringue
4 eggs, beaten
8 Tbsp (¼ lb) unsalted butter, cut into pats

Meringue

4 egg whites
Pinch cream of tartar
⅓ cup sugar
¼ tsp vanilla extract

The Crust

✦ *Preheat oven to 425°F.*

Prepare pastry for a single-crust pie. Line a regular 9-inch pie tin with the pastry. Work the pastry into a collar that stands above the rim and flute the edge. Prick the bottom of the crust with a fork so it does not bubble up during baking. Line the pie shell with aluminum foil or baking paper and fill it with dried beans or rice. Bake in a preheated 425° oven for 15 minutes. Remove the foil and beans, bake for a further 15 minutes. Remove from the oven and cool to room temperature.

The Lemon Filling

✦ Place the lemon juice, sugar, zest, yolks, eggs, and butter in the top of a double boiler. Cook over simmering water, stirring constantly, until the mixture thickens. It should be the consistency of yogurt. Pour into the pie shell and smooth the surface.

The Meringue

✦ Avoid making meringue in hot, humid weather or on a rainy day. Airborne water reacts with the sugar in the meringue, turning the mixture into a soft, sticky mess. Lemon meringue pie is best if eaten the day it is made. Uneaten pie should be refrigerated even though this will cause the meringue to "weep."

Whip the egg whites with a pinch of cream of tartar until they barely show signs of soft peaks. Gradually pour in the sugar. Beat the meringue until it holds soft peaks. It should be neither stiff nor dry. Fold in the vanilla extract. Spread over the lemon filling and make small peaks with a spatula. Put the pie into a preheated 325° oven for 20–25 minutes or until the meringue is well colored and slightly crisp on the surface. Cool to room temperature before serving.

Elmore Mountain Apple Pie

Yield 8 servings

Elmore Mountain Apple Pie is named for the ridge where I have my home. I like to use old-fashioned pie apples, my favorite being Duchess from a dooryard tree. Subtly flavored with spices and maple sugar, apple pie is perfect for any meal, especially breakfast, with a wedge of sharp Cheddar cheese.

No two apple pies are alike, partly because each variety has its own characteristics. The best apples for pies are Alexander, Baldwin, Cortland, Duchess, Dudley, Granny Smith, Jonathan, Northwestern, Greening, Pumpkin (Pound) Sweet, Rhode Island Greening, Rome Beauty, Stayman Winesap, Tolman Sweet, Tompkins King, and Wolf River. For more about apples, see Chapter 1, Vermont Ingredients: Apples.

Apples dry out in storage. By February or March it is usually necessary to add a couple of tablespoons of cider to replace the moisture lost to evaporation. Old storage apples can cause a stiff, dry pie.

Pastry for a double-crust pie
1 egg, separated
1 Tbsp water

The Filling

8 cups pie apples, peeled, cored, and sliced
½ cup maple or brown sugar
2 Tbsp cornstarch
1 tsp cinnamon
Good grating fresh nutmeg
Pinch allspice
2 Tbsp butter

✦ Roll out and line a 9–10-inch, deep-dish pie tin with half the pastry. Keep the remaining pastry wrapped and refrigerated until required. Beat the egg white lightly and use it to paint the inside of the pie shell. Prick the crust with a fork in several places and refrigerate until ready to fill.
Preheat oven to 400°F.

Place the prepared apples in a large bowl. In a separate bowl mix the maple sugar, cornstarch, and spices. Toss with the apples until evenly coated and pile into the prepared pastry. Settle the apples by pushing down on them to remove air pockets and voids. This prevents airspace between apples and crust. Dot the filling with the butter.

Roll out the remaining pastry, wrap it around the rolling pin, and unroll onto the pie. Seal with cold water, and flute the edge. Mix the egg yolk with a tablespoon of water. Paint the top crust lightly with some of the mixture. Make several small gashes in the crust to allow steam to escape.

Bake on the bottom shelf of a preheated 400° oven for 50–55 minutes or until nicely browned and the pie is bubbly in the center. Cool for at least 1 hour before serving. Serve with sharp Cheddar cheese and half-whipped cream.

Cheese and Buttermilk Pie
Yield 10–12 servings

A cross between cheesecake and custard pie, this dessert has an old-fashioned flavor heightened by a touch of cider vinegar. Vary the pie by lining the shell with several tablespoons of fruit preserves—apricot, peach, or apple butter are best.

Pastry for a single-crust pie
1 egg white

Filling
   8 oz cream cheese
   2 Tbsp cornstarch
   ½ cup sugar
   2½ cups buttermilk, preferably labeled *churned* on the container
   4 eggs, beaten
   1 tsp vanilla extract
   1 Tbsp cider vinegar

✦ Line a 10-inch, deep-dish pie tin with the pastry. Work up a collar that stands above the rim and flute the edge. Beat the egg white and use it to paint the inside of the pie shell. Prick the pastry in several places with a fork. Refrigerate until ready to fill.

Preheat oven to 325°F.   *(Continued)*

Beat the cream cheese, cornstarch, and sugar in the bowl of an electric mixer at medium speed, using the paddle attachment. When combined, gradually pour in the buttermilk and beat until smooth. Pour in the eggs, vanilla, vinegar, and beat until smooth, about 2 minutes.

Place the pie shell on the bottom shelf rack of the oven and then pour the mixture into the pie shell. This is much easier than trying to carry a 10-inch plate of the liquid filling across the kitchen. Bake in the preheated 325° oven for 70 minutes or until the center of the pie has set. Test for doneness by jiggling the pie plate. When the filling stays put and appears firm, it is done. Bake only until the pie is set; if it is puffed in the center, it will be grainy and fissures will appear as the pie cools. Cool completely to room temperature before serving. This pie is best if served the day it is made. Refrigerate any uneaten pie.

Deep Dish Pumpkin Pie
Yield 10–12 servings

The harvest dinner, a New England community tradition, marks summer's passing and celebrates the bounty of its fruits. Spicy pumpkin pie topped with plenty of whipped cream provides a grand finale for any foliage season supper.

Pastry for a single-crust pie
2 Tbsp apricot jam

Filling

2 cups pumpkin puree or one can prepared pumpkin filling
1 cup heavy cream
½ cup maple syrup
½ cup light brown sugar
4 eggs, beaten
½ tsp salt
½ tsp cinnamon
½ tsp ginger
½ tsp nutmeg

✦ Line a 9–10-inch, deep-dish pie tin with the pastry. Work up a collar that stands above the rim and flute the edge. Melt the jam and paint the inside of the pie shell. Prick the crust with a fork in several places. Refrigerate until ready to fill.

Preheat oven to 350°F.

Cook enough pumpkin or squash to yield 2 cups of smooth puree. Combine the pumpkin, cream, syrup, sugar, salt, and spices in a bowl and mix until smooth. Add the beaten eggs and continue to whisk until homogenous.

Place the pie shell on the bottom shelf rack of a preheated 350° oven and then pour the filling into the shell. This is much easier than trying to carry a dish full of liquid filling across the kitchen. Bake for 60–70 minutes or until the center of the pie has set. Test by jiggling the dish to see if the filling stays put and appears firm. Bake only until the pie has set. If it is fully puffed in the center, it will be dry and grainy in texture and fissures will appear as the pie cools. Cool completely to room temperature before slicing so that the pie may set. If you wish to serve the pie warm, do so by reheating for a few minutes. Serve with whipped cream flavored with rum or applejack. This pie is best if served the day it is made. Refrigerate any uneaten pie.

Peach Pie
Yield 8 servings

Line the pie shell with raspberry jam to keep the bottom crust crisp, flavor the peaches, and suggest the famous Melba blend of peaches and raspberries. A crunchy coating of cinnamon sugar gives the top crust its sheen.

Pastry for a lattice-top pie
¼ cup raspberry jam

The Filling
3 lb fresh peaches
½ cup sugar
4 Tbsp cornstarch
Juice 1 lemon   *(Continued)*

Topping
⅛ tsp cinnamon
1 tsp sugar

✦ Line a regular 9-inch pie tin with half the pastry. Refrigerate until ready to fill.

Preheat oven to 400°F.

Bring a large pot of water to a boil. Plunge the peaches into the water, a few at a time, so that the water continues to boil. Leave the peaches in the boiling water for 15–20 seconds. Remove with a slotted spoon and plunge into ice water. Continue the process until all the peaches have been treated. Skin the fruit and remove the stones. Slice the peaches into a bowl and squeeze lemon juice over them. Combine the sugar and cornstarch in another bowl. Toss with the peaches to coat them evenly.

Spread the raspberry jam over the inside of the pie shell. Prick the shell in a few places with a fork. Pile in the filling and dampen the edge of the crust with cold water.

Roll out the remaining pastry and cut into strips ½ inch wide. Place parallel strips ½ inch apart across the pie. Place perpendicular strips, starting in the center and working to either side, weaving as you go. Trim the excess crust and flute the edge. Mix together the cinnamon and sugar and sprinkle over the lattice crust. Bake on the bottom shelf of a preheated 400° oven for 50 minutes or until the crust is golden brown and the filling bubbles up in the center of the pie. Cool at least 1 hour before serving.

Strawberry Rhubarb Pie with Crumb Topping
Yield 8 servings

Rhubarb appears in early spring, sometimes so early it pokes through patches of wet snow. "Pie plant," as it is also known, and early strawberries are a wonderful combination. Freshly squeezed orange juice and a cinnamon crumb topping enhance this version of an old favorite.

Pastry for a single-crust pie
2 Tbsp currant jelly

Filling

2 cups young, tender rhubarb, peeled, in ½-inch cubes
2 cups strawberries, hulled and sliced
½ cup sugar
3 Tbsp cornstarch
Juice of one orange or ¼ cup orange juice

Topping

⅓ cup all-purpose flour
3 Tbsp light brown sugar
½ tsp cinnamon
2 Tbsp butter, melted

✦ Line a regular 9-inch pie tin with the pastry. Work up a collar that stands above the rim and flute the edge. Melt the currant jelly and use it to paint the inside of the pie shell. Prick the crust with a fork in several places. Refrigerate until ready to fill.

Preheat oven to 400°F.

Put the diced rhubarb into a bowl with the sliced strawberries and orange juice. In a separate bowl, stir together the cornstarch and sugar. Toss with the filling until the rhubarb and berries are well coated. Pour into the pie shell.

The Topping

✦ Stir together the flour, sugar, and cinnamon. Add the melted butter and work with your hands until the mixture resembles lumpy cornmeal. Sprinkle an even layer over the pie. Bake on the bottom shelf of a pre-heated 400° oven 45–50 minutes or until the pie is bubbly and the topping is browned. Cool to room temperature before slicing.

Blueberry Pie
Yield 8 servings

A touch of orange juice and cloves accents the naturally spicy flavor of the blueberries.

Pastry for a double-crust pie
1 egg separated
1 Tbsp water

The Filling

5 cups blueberries
½ cup sugar
4 Tbsp cornstarch
Pinch ground cloves
Juice of one small orange (¼ cup orange juice)

✦ Line a tin with half the pastry. Keep the remaining pastry wrapped and refrigerated until required. Beat the egg white lightly and use it to paint the inside of the pie shell. Prick the crust with a fork in several places.

Preheat oven to 400°F.

Pick over the berries to remove stems and leaves. Wash them and drain well. Place the blueberries in a bowl with the orange juice. In a separate bowl rub together the sugar, cornstarch, and cloves. Toss with the berries until evenly coated. Pile the mixture into the prepared pie shell. Dampen the edge with water.

Roll out the remaining pastry. Wrap around the rolling pin and unroll onto the pie. Trim the excess dough and seal and flute the edge. Mix together the egg yolk with the water and paint the top of the pie. Make 3–4 small gashes in the crust to allow the steam to escape.

Bake on the bottom shelf of a preheated 400° oven for 50 minutes or until the pie is nicely browned and bubbly in the center. Cool to room temperature before slicing. If you want to serve the pie warm, it is better to reheat after it has set.

Cherry and Almond Tart
Yield 8 servings

The sour cherry thrives in the north, where temperatures regularly fall below zero. Rugged and small, the tree grows in places well beyond the range of the sweet cherry. Its fruit is tart and best suited for cooking. This dessert, a large almond cookie filled with clear red pie-cherries flavored with cinnamon and almonds, is absolutely delicious.

The Crust

1 cup unbleached all-purpose flour
½ cup almonds, ground fine
1 tsp baking powder
¼ tsp salt
4 Tbsp unsalted butter, softened
2 egg yolks, reserve whites
2½ tsp almond liqueur

The Filling

2 lb sour cherries (fresh, drained if frozen or canned)
½ cup sugar
1 Tbsp cornstarch
½ tsp cinnamon
¼ tsp almond extract

The Topping

½ cup slivered almonds
1 Tbsp sugar

The Crust

✦ Toast 1 cup of slivered almonds in a 400° oven 5–7 minutes or until lightly colored. Using a food processor, grind half the toasted almonds to a fine powder. Reserve the remaining nuts for the topping.

Sift together the flour, sugar, ground almonds, salt, and baking powder. Stir them together with a fork to make sure the ingredients are well distributed. Add the butter, yolks, and almond liqueur. Work into a pliable dough.

This is really a type of cookie dough so it cannot be rolled out like regular pie pastry. Gather the pastry into a ball and then flatten it into a disc. Line 9-inch tart pan with the dough. Model the pastry with your fingers and a flat-bottomed drinking glass to an even thickness. Brush the inside of the tart shell with some of the reserved egg white to seal it from the fruit filling. Prick it with a fork in a dozen or so places. Refrigerate until ready to fill.

Preheat oven to 375°F.

Stem and pit the cherries and toss with the almond extract. In a separate bowl combine the sugar, cornstarch, and cinnamon; toss with the cherries to coat evenly. Pile the cherry mixture into the tart shell. Press down with the flat of your hand to expel as much air as possible. Sprinkle with the toasted almonds and then the sugar. Bake on the center shelf of a preheated 375° oven 45–50 minutes or until bubbly in the center. Cool for at least 1 hour before serving.

Chocolate Cake with Raspberry Buttercream
Yield 12 servings

There are plenty of calories in this moist, very rich, very dark chocolate cake. Nevertheless, it is the most requested cake in my repertoire.

The Cake

4 oz unsweetened baking chocolate
1 cup water
2 cups light brown sugar
1 cup unsalted butter (½ lb), softened
1 tsp vanilla extract
3 eggs
1½ cups unbleached all-purpose flour
½ tsp salt
1 tsp baking soda

The Filling

1 cup raspberry jam

The Frosting

2 egg yolks
1 cup red raspberry jam
1 cup unsalted butter (½ lb), softened

✦ Chop the chocolate into pea-sized pieces, put into a saucepan with the water, and place on very low heat. Stir the chocolate occasionally so it does not stick to the pan. Once melted, remove from the heat and leave to rest for 5 minutes. It should be quite thick and smooth, the consistency of hot fudge sauce.

Preheat oven to 350°F.

Beat the brown sugar and butter in an electric mixer with the paddle attachment until lightened. Add the eggs, one at a time, turning the machine off and scraping down the sides of the bowl before the addition of each egg. Beat until light and fluffy, about 3 minutes and add the vanilla extract.

In a separate bowl sift together the flour, salt, and baking soda. Stir them with a fork to make sure the ingredients are well distributed. Set the mixer on low speed. Alternate adding the flour and melted chocolate to the batter, beginning and ending with the flour. Beat until just combined. There should be no visible spots of flour, but be careful, for overbeating can cause a tough cake.

Pour the batter into two greased and floured 9-inch cake pans with removable bottoms. Line the pans with waxed paper if they do not have removable bottoms. Bake on the center shelf of a preheated 350° oven for 50 minutes. The cake should be slightly puffed in the center. Test for doneness by inserting a cake tester into the center of the cake, which is done if the tester comes out clean. Allow the cakes to cool to room temperature before removing from the pans.

When the cakes are cool, put one of the layers on a platter and spread with the raspberry jam. Place the other layer on top.

The Frosting

✦ Place the red raspberry jam and the yolks in the top of a double boiler set over simmering water. Heat, stirring constantly, until the mixture thickens and will hold soft peaks. Remove from the heat and cool to room temperature. Pour into the bowl of an electric mixer and whip until lightened in color and volume. Add the butter a little at a time and continue to whip until fluffy.

Spread a thin layer of the frosting all over the cake to seal the crumbs. Use the remainder for frosting and decoration. Garnish the cake with fresh raspberries and mint leaves. Serve at room temperature. This cake should be kept refrigerated, but plan to remove from the refrigerator about 2 hours before serving.

Spiced Apple Cake with Maple Frosting
Yield 12 servings

Based on a classic combination—apples, maple syrup, and spices—this rich, moist cake is wonderful served by the fireside on a cold day. For an extra lift, accompany it with snifters of "Sugarbush Spirits," a new Vermont product distilled from maple syrup.

The Cake

1 cup (½ lb) unsalted butter, softened
1½ cups light brown sugar
2 eggs
1½ cups applesauce
1 tsp vanilla extract
2½ cups unbleached all-purpose flour
½ cup graham flour
1 tsp cinnamon
½ tsp nutmeg, freshly grated
½ tsp ground ginger
½ tsp ground allspice
½ tsp salt
1½ tsp baking powder
1 tsp baking soda
1 cup cooking apples, small dice
½ cup chopped walnuts
1 cup raisins, chopped

The Syrup

⅓ cup maple syrup, preferably dark amber
2 Tbsp dark rum (optional)

The Frosting

1½ cups maple syrup, preferably dark amber
3 large egg yolks
1 cup (½ lb) unsalted butter, softened
Walnut halves for decoration

The Cake

✦ *Preheat oven to 350°F.*

Place the butter and sugar in the bowl of an electric mixer. Blend, using the paddle attachment, until smooth and light. Add the eggs, one at a time, and beat at high speed until fluffy. Add the vanilla.

Sift together the flours, spices, salt, baking powder, and baking soda. Stir the sifted ingredients with a fork to distribute the ingredients well. In a separate bowl toss the chopped apples, raisins, and walnuts with a spoonful of the flour mixture. This helps keep them suspended in the batter.

Set the mixer on the lowest speed. Add the flour and applesauce alternately, starting and ending with the flour. Scrape down the sides of the bowl and beat just until the batter is smooth. Fold the raisin mixture into the batter with a spatula. Pour the batter into two 9-inch cake tins that have been greased and floured. Line the bottoms of the tins with waxed paper if they do not have removable bottoms.

Bake on the center shelf of a preheated 350° oven for 40 minutes or until a cake tester inserted into the center of the cake comes out clean. Cool the cakes completely before removing from tins.

The Syrup

✦ Heat the ⅓ cup of maple syrup until it just comes to a boil. Remove from the heat and stir in the rum. Brush the top of each layer until all this syrup has been absorbed.

The Frosting

✦ Pour the 1½ cups of maple syrup into a saucepan and simmer over low heat until a candy thermometer registers 232° (late thread stage), the temperature used for sugar on snow. Keep an eye on the pot; if the heat is too high, it will boil over.

While the syrup is simmering, put the yolks in the bowl of an electric mixer and whip until lightened in color and volume. Remove the syrup from the heat. Pour very slowly into the yolks while the machine is running. Run the machine until the mixture is fluffy and has cooled to room temperature. Add the butter gradually, in walnut-size pieces, and whip until the frosting is very light.

Do not attempt to frost until the cake has completely cooled or the frosting will melt on contact, like butter on toast. Fill the cake with some of the frosting. Spread the remaining frosting over the sides and top. Garnish the top with walnut halves and serve at room temperature.

Strawberry Shortcake
Yield 10 servings

An old-fashioned version of the traditional Fourth-of-July favorite. Split a large buttermilk cake, fill it with berries and syrup, and crown it with half-whipped cream and more berries. A stunning presentation, it proves once again that the simplest foods are often the best.

The Filling

2 qt strawberries, hulled and sliced thick
1 cup sugar
4 Tbsp strawberry or orange liqueur (optional)

The Shortcake

2 cups unbleached all-purpose flour
1 cup cake flour
1 tsp salt
4 tsp baking powder
½ tsp baking soda
2 Tbsp sugar
½ cup shortening or lard, chilled
1 cup buttermilk
6 Tbsp unsalted butter, softened (for use when assembling the shortcake)

The Topping

1 cup heavy cream, whipped to soft peaks

The Filling

✦ Wash and drain the berries before hulling. Toss the berries, sugar, and liqueur in a bowl, cover, and refrigerate at least 4 hours before serving. The berries will make plenty of syrup, which will ultimately be absorbed by the thirsty layers of tender shortcake.

The Shortcake

✦ *Preheat oven to 400°F.*

Sift together the flours, salt, baking powder, baking soda, and sugar into a mixing bowl. Stir them with a fork to ensure even distribution of ingredients. Cut the lard or shortening into the flour with a pastry cutter or a fork until the mixture resembles cornmeal. Pour in the buttermilk and work quickly into a soft, sticky dough.

Pat the dough directly into a greased and floured 9-inch cake pan. Bake on the center shelf of a preheated 400° oven for 35 minutes. Cool before removing from the pan.

The Topping

✦ Whip the cream only until it forms soft peaks; it should flow slightly when mounded on the shortcake. Do not sweeten it. The cream should provide contrast to the sweetness of the berries.

Assembling the Strawberry Shortcake

✦ Slice the shortcake in half and spread the butter on the cut sides. Place the bottom layer, butter side up, on an oven-proof serving platter. Cover with half of the strawberries and syrup. Cover with the top layer, butter side down. Place in a 400° oven for 5 minutes.

Remove from the oven, top with the remaining berries and syrup, and then the whipped cream. Spoon a few of the strawberries on top of the cream as a crowning touch. Present at the table and cut into wedges.

Variations

2 qt fresh raspberries
1 cup sugar
4 Tbsp raspberry or orange liqueur (optional)

3 lb fresh peaches, peeled and sliced
1 cup sugar
½ tsp cinnamon
4 Tbsp orange liqueur (optional)

Creamy Rice Pudding

Yield 8–10 servings

The key to this creamy pudding is short-grained rice, which becomes very soft and almost falls apart in the light cream. Whipped egg whites, folded into the pudding, rise to the surface during baking and form a foamy layer flecked with rum-soaked raisins.

1 cup short-grained rice. Do not use long-grained or preprocessed rice, both of which make a poor rice pudding. Short-grained Italian Arborio rice is perfect, and Asian varieties also work well.
3 cups water
½ tsp salt
3 eggs, separated
1 cup white sugar
Juice ½ lemon (2 Tbsp lemon juice)
1 tsp vanilla extract
2 cups light cream
½ cup raisins
¼ cup dark rum, or ¼ cup cider
Grating fresh nutmeg

✦ Put the raisins and rum into a saucepan, cover, and heat just to boiling. Remove from the heat and leave to let the raisins absorb the rum, about 45 minutes.

Preheat oven to 350°F.

Put the water and salt into a saucepan, bring to a boil, and add the rice. Cover tightly and cook over low heat until all the water has been absorbed, about 50 minutes. The rice should be very soft and sticky.

Beat the yolks and sugar with an electric mixer until light in color. Pour in the cream, beat for 2 minutes, and add the lemon juice and vanilla. In a separate bowl beat the egg whites to soft peaks. Mix the cream and rice together and fold in the whites. Pour into a buttered baking dish, sprinkle the raisins on top, and grate some nutmeg over the surface.

Place the dish containing the pudding into a larger pan. Add hot water to come halfway up the sides of the pudding dish. Bake on the center shelf of a preheated 350° oven for 50 minutes or until golden brown and the center has set. Test for doneness by jiggling the baking dish. The pudding is done if it does not move in the center.

Remove from the oven and let rest for at least 15 minutes before serving. Rice pudding is best served warm or room temperature on the day it is made. Refrigerate any uneaten pudding.

Indian Pudding Soufflé
Yield 6 servings

The dark glowing flavor of Indian pudding is incorporated into this airy soufflé. The result is a light dessert that suggests centuries of tradition. Serve with sweetened whipped cream or vanilla ice cream.

½ cup cornmeal (preferably stone ground)
1 tsp ground cinnamon
1 tsp ground ginger
½ tsp nutmeg, grated
½ tsp salt
2 cups milk
½ cup molasses
¼ cup brown sugar
4 Tbsp unsalted butter
4 eggs, separated
Confectioner's sugar for garnish

✦ Stir the cornmeal, spices, and salt together. Combine with the milk, molasses, butter, and sugar in the top of a double boiler. Cook over simmering water for 20 minutes, stirring occasionally. The pudding should be quite thick and dark in color.

Remove from the heat and stir the yolks into the pudding, one at a time. Return to the heat and cook for several minutes, stirring all the while. Cook until the pudding is smooth and has regained its former thickness. Remove from the heat and continue to stir for 1 minute. Cool to room temperature before proceeding with the recipe. The soufflé can be made up to this point before you begin preparing dinner. Fold in the whites and bake when you are ready.

Preheat oven to 375°F.

Prepare a 1½- or 2-quart soufflé dish by buttering it lightly and dusting with powdered sugar. Put it in a slightly warm place so that you are not pouring your soufflé into a dish still cold from the pantry.   *(Continued)*

Beat the egg whites with a pinch of salt to soft peaks. Stir one-third of them into the pudding to lighten it. Fold the remaining whites into the mixture so that the whites retain their volume.

Pour the mixture into the prepared dish. Bake on the center shelf of a preheated 375° oven for 45 minutes. The soufflé will be the color of roasted chestnuts and will have risen several inches above the rim of the dish. Dust with a cloud of confectioner's sugar and rush to the table and serve immediately.

Butternut Cookies
Yield 2 dozen cookies

Butternut trees are common in the northeast. Their range extends northward well past the limits of the walnut, a relative. Similar to the walnut in many respects, the butternut is oval in shape and has a certain richness and flavor that distinguishes it from all other nuts. Because it grows wild throughout the state, it is as familiar to Vermonters as maple syrup. Serve with ice creams, custards, baked apples, or all by themselves.

½ cup (¼ lb) unsalted butter, softened
½ cup maple or light brown sugar
3 eggs
½ tsp vanilla extract
1 Tbsp sherry
1 cup unbleached all-purpose flour
½ cup butternuts, ground fine; walnuts may be substituted
Butternuts as garnish

✦ To shell butternuts, pour boiling water to cover nuts, let sit for 15 minutes, open nuts with a nutcracker.

Preheat oven to 400°F.

Put the butter and sugar into the bowl of an electric mixer. Beat, using the paddle attachment, until lightened in color and volume. Add the eggs, one at a time. Turn off the machine and scrape down the sides of the bowl before the addition of each egg. Beat until fluffy; add the vanilla and sherry.

Sift the flour and rub the ground nuts into it with your hands. Fold the flour into the butter mixture, working it just long enough so there are no visible spots of flour. Drop tablespoonsful of the batter onto a greased and floured sheet pan. Press a butternut, or several large pieces, into the top of each. Bake on the center shelf of a preheated 400° oven for 15 minutes or until the cookies are golden brown around the edges and lightly colored on top.

Ice Creams and Sherbets

✦

Raspberry Sherbet

Mulled Cider Sherbet

Pear Sherbet

Strawberry Sherbet

Peach Sherbet

Blueberry Sherbet

Maple Walnut Ice Cream

Clover Honey Ice Cream

Chocolate Ice Cream

Strawberry Ice Cream

Strawberry Ice Cream with Brown Sugar and Sour Cream

Peach Praline Ice Cream

Pumpkin Ice Cream

How to Make Ice Creams and Sherbets

Motor-driven freezers can produce fine ice creams and sherbets. There's a certain satisfaction that comes from hand-cranking ice cream, but both means come to the same end.

I have used many different freezers, both manual and electric, and I prefer the old-fashioned "paddle in canister" variety that uses ice and salt as the freezing medium. This type is more reliable and produces better results. Models range from 2-quart to 20-quart capacity. For home use I recommend a canister that holds 4–6 quarts. I particularly like the New England-made White Mountain brand freezers.

Look for a solid, heavily built model that will stand years of abuse. The canister must be made of metal—plastic has no thermal conductivity. Tall, narrow ones are better than short, squat models because their long, thin shape provides more surface area and less width, and thus they require a shorter freezing time.

Paddles made from metal or a combination of metal and wood will last longer and prove more reliable than those made of plastic. Motors should be powerful and well sealed to prevent exposure to salt. The bucket should serve as an insulator to prevent the ice from melting. Pine and oak are popular materials; better models employ tongue-and-groove construction.

Ice creams and sherbets are frozen in the same manner. It is the ingredients that make the difference. Ice creams, usually much richer, use heavy cream, egg yolks, and sugar. The addition of flavoring, fruits, spices, chocolate, nuts, candy, crumbled cookies, or "the works" produces delectable variations.

Sherbets, in the purest sense, consist of pureed fruit or fruit juice and sugar syrup. This purest version has come to be known in this country as sorbet, which is simply the French word for sherbet. Sherbets can be made with milk and egg whites, but these additions reduce the clarity of the flavors.

Few things can go wrong with frozen desserts. It is easy to correct those that do. For ice creams make sure the custard is cooked and well thickened to avoid an eggy taste. Strain the cooked custard to ensure smoothness. Always be patient. Wait until the base has chilled before adding the fruit, unless the recipe directs otherwise. Start with a chilled mixture in the canister. This saves freezing time and ice.

Most machines do not require crushed ice. Regular-size cubes will produce satisfactory results. Irregularly shaped pieces do have better freezing potential because they pack in tighter, so a once-over with a mallet or rolling pin can speed results. However, this is not an essential step.

Place the filled canister in the bucket and surround it with ice and salt. Table salt will work, but coarse-grained rock or kosher salt provides more uniform ice/salt distribution. Plan on using 1 cup of salt per gallon of ice. Layer ice, then salt, then more ice in three installments until the bucket is full to the top of the canister. Replenish the ice as it melts until your ice cream or sherbet is thick and clings to the paddle in a block that just holds its shape.

The mixture requires 20–40 minutes to freeze. If it freezes in less time, you have used too much salt and your dessert will be grainy. If this occurs, allow the mixture to melt in your refrigerator and refreeze using less salt. If the mixture is unfrozen after 45 minutes, you have not used enough salt. Simply add more salt and run the machine until it sets. If you plan to add liquor to the dessert, wait until the ice cream blocks around the paddle. Add the liquor and run the machine just long enough to distribute it evenly.

Once the ice cream sets, you can remove the dessert from the canister and pack it into containers to freeze in your household freezer. Or, you can remove the cranking device from the canister, cork the hole, repack the bucket with ice and more salt, and serve the frozen dessert directly from the canister—a nice touch at a barbecue.

If the ice cream or sherbet freezes too hard to serve, it didn't have enough air worked into it and will be heavy. Next time allow the machine to run a bit longer and remove the mixture only after it blocks around the paddle. Always allow the ice cream or sherbet to soften in your refrigerator 20 minutes before serving. The slight softening releases the flavor and texture.

Raspberry Sherbet
Yield 1 quart

If you've never tasted homemade sherbet, this one will be a revelation. Frozen berries do just as well in this recipe so it can be a year-round treat. Substitute blackberries, boysenberries, or similar fruits for raspberries for a change of pace.

1½ cups sugar
1 cup water
3 cups pureed raspberries (1 quart fresh berries or 3½ cups berries that have been frozen and thawed; do not drain)

✦ Put the sugar and water in a saucepan. Bring to a boil and simmer until the syrup is clear, about 1 minute. Remove from the heat and chill before proceeding with the recipe.

Puree the berries and pass them through a wire strainer to extract the seeds. There are about ½ cup of seeds in a quart of raspberries. Pour the pureed berries and chilled syrup into an ice-cream freezer. Freeze according to the manufacturer's directions.

When it is thick and blocks around the paddle, spoon the sherbet into a mold or freezer container. Seal it tightly and place in your household freezer for several hours until frozen. The sherbet will be at its best if you transfer it to your refrigerator 20 minutes before serving, to soften it slightly.

Mulled Cider Sherbet
Yield about 1½ quarts

This frozen version of hot, spiced apple cider is as refreshing in summer as it is in winter.

1 qt sweet cider
2 cups sugar
1 stick cinnamon
6 cloves
6 allspice berries
Grating fresh nutmeg
2 Tbsp dark rum

✦ Heat the cider, sugar, and spices in a saucepan until steaming but do not allow the mixture to boil. Cool to room temperature; then pour through a wire strainer to remove the spices. Pour the mulled cider into the canister of an ice cream freezer. Freeze according to the manufacturer's instructions. When the sherbet is thick and clings to the paddle in a block, add the rum and run the machine just long enough to incorporate it into the mixture. Spoon the sherbet into a freezer container and place in your household freezer for several hours until frozen.

The rum keeps this sherbet creamy and spoonable so there is no need to soften it in your refrigerator before serving.

Pear Sherbet

Yield 1½ quarts

Pear sherbet is creamy and subtle. I don't know why it is such a rarity. No matter, homemade is better than storebought any day.

1½ cups sugar
1 cup water
3 lb fresh, ripe pears
1 Tbsp lemon juice

✦ The pears should be soft to the touch and fragrant. Unripe pears will produce a grainy result no matter how long you cook them.

Peel, core, and quarter the pears and place them in a saucepan with the remaining ingredients. Cover the pears and simmer over low heat until the fruit has softened or 20–30 minutes.

Puree the cooked pears with the syrup in a blender or food processor. Pour the puree into the canister of an ice-cream freezer. Freeze according to the manufacturer's instructions.

When it is thick and clings to the paddle, spoon the sherbet into a mold or freezer container. Seal tightly and place in your household freezer for several hours until frozen. For peak flavor transfer the sherbet to your refrigerator 20 minutes before serving. This allows it to soften and to release its flavor.

Strawberry Sherbet
Yield about 1 quart

Simple ingredients produce an intense flavor and a fiery red color.

1½ cups sugar
1 cup water
1 Tbsp lemon juice
1 qt fresh strawberries or 3½ cups berries that have been frozen and thawed; do not drain

✦ Put the sugar and water in a saucepan, bring to a boil, and simmer until the syrup is clear, about 1 minute. Remove from the heat and chill before proceeding with the recipe. If the syrup is not completely cool, the strawberries will react adversely to the heat, turn gray, and lose their fresh flavor.

Wash and drain the berries, and when they are dry, hull them. Puree in a blender or food processor with the chilled syrup and lemon juice. Pour into the canister of an ice-cream freezer and freeze according to the manufacturer's instructions.

When the sherbet is thick and clings to the paddle in a block, spoon into a mold or freezer container. Seal tightly and place in your household freezer for several hours until frozen. For peak flavor transfer the sherbet to your refrigerator 20 minutes before serving.

Peach Sherbet
Yield 1½ quarts

Canned peaches packed in syrup work well in this sherbet, but, of course, they don't compete with fresh summer produce. Simply pour the contents of the can into a blender, puree, and process in an ice-cream freezer. If you crave this sherbet during the winter months, this is the best path to follow. I have never had a decent imported peach during the winter.

1½ cups sugar
1 cup water
3 lb fresh, ripe peaches, or two 29-oz cans
2 Tbsp lemon juice

✦ Put the sugar and water in a saucepan. Bring to a boil and simmer until the syrup is clear, about 1 minute. Remove from the heat and chill before proceeding with the recipe.

Bring a large pot of water to a boil. Plunge the peaches into it, a few at a time, so the water continues to boil. Leave the fruit in the boiling water 15–20 seconds. Remove with a slotted spoon and immerse in cold water. Slip the skins from the peaches and remove the stones.

Puree the peaches in a blender or processor with the syrup and lemon juice. Pour into the canister of an ice-cream freezer and freeze according to the manufacturer's instructions.

When it is thick and clings to the paddle in a block, spoon the sherbet into a mold or freezer container. Seal tightly and place in your household freezer for several hours until frozen. For peak flavor, transfer the sherbet to your refrigerator for 20 minutes before serving so that it softens slightly.

Blueberry Sherbet
Yield 1 quart

Make this sherbet with uncooked berries or with berries cooked in the syrup. The cooked berries produce a deep blue sherbet with a flavor that suggests blueberry pie. Sherbet made from fresh, raw berries tastes quite different and is much lighter in color. It is hard to say which is better.

1½ cups sugar
1 cup water
1 qt fresh blueberries
Juice 1 orange

✦ Put the sugar and water in a saucepan. Bring to a boil and simmer until the syrup is clear, about 1 minute. Remove from the heat and chill before proceeding with the recipe.

Puree the blueberries in a blender with the syrup and orange juice until very smooth. Pour the puree into the canister of an ice-cream freezer and freeze according to the manufacturer's instructions.

When the sherbet is thick and blocks around the paddle, spoon it into a mold or freezer container. Place in your household freezer for several hours until frozen. For peak flavor, transfer the sherbet to the refrigerator 20 minutes before serving.

Maple Walnut Ice Cream
Yield 2 quarts

Few visitors to Vermont can resist this combination—a favorite with residents.

3 cups milk
10 egg yolks
2 cups maple syrup
2 cups heavy cream
1 cup chopped walnuts

✦ Put the milk into a saucepan and heat slowly until steaming. Have the yolks at hand in a stainless steel bowl. Using a ladle slowly pour some of the hot milk into the bowl with the yolks and whisk together. Now the yolks can be added to the milk in the saucepan. Pour them slowly into the milk, whisking all the while. Cook over low heat until the custard coats the back of a spoon, or just below the point of boiling. Be careful not to spoil the custard by boiling it. Remove from the heat and pour through a wire strainer into a bowl. Add the maple syrup and stir together. Cover and refrigerate until chilled.

Whip the heavy cream to soft peaks and fold into the maple custard. Pour into the canister of an ice-cream freezer and freeze according to the manufacturer's instructions.

When it has thickened and clings to the paddle in a block, the ice cream is done. Add the walnuts and run the machine just long enough to distribute them through the mixture. Spoon the ice cream into a container to freeze in your household freezer or remove the cranking device, cork the top of the canister, repack the bucket with ice and salt, and serve later directly from the canister.

Clover Honey Ice Cream
Yield 2 quarts

Red clover grows abundantly in New England. Found along roadsides and in pastures, this familiar plant has been honored as Vermont's state flower. The nectar from its round purplish-red blossoms produces a light, delicately flavored honey, sweeter than sugar.

1 qt milk
½ cup clover honey
1 cup sugar
2 vanilla beans
10 egg yolks
2 cups heavy cream

✦ Put the milk, honey, sugar, and vanilla beans into a saucepan, and heat slowly until steaming. Remove from heat and let stand for 15 minutes. Remove the vanilla beans and reserve for another use. Have the yolks at hand in a stainless steel bowl. Using a ladle, slowly pour some of the hot milk into the bowl with the yolks and whisk together. Now the yolks can be added to the milk in the saucepan. Pour them slowly into the milk, whisking all the while. Return to the heat and cook slowly over a low flame until the custard coats the back of a spoon, or just below the point of boiling. Be careful not to spoil the custard by boiling it. Pour the custard through a wire strainer into a bowl. Cover and refrigerate until chilled.

Whip the heavy cream to soft peaks and fold into the custard. Pour the custard into the canister of an ice cream freezer and freeze according to the manufacturer's instructions. When it is thickened and clings to the paddle in a block, spoon the ice-cream into a container to freeze in your household freezer, or remove the cranking device, cork the top of the canister, repack the bucket with ice and salt, leave until set, and serve directly from the canister.

Chocolate Ice Cream
Yield 2½ quarts

Try this at a birthday party. Do the preliminary work ahead. The celebrants will enjoy watching the canister spin in the ice and anticipating the delectable results.

1 qt milk
2 cups sugar
10 egg yolks
1 lb dark chocolate, chopped fine; or 1 lb semisweet chocolate chips
⅛ tsp powdered mace
2 tsp vanilla extract
2 cups heavy cream

✦ Put the milk, sugar, and mace into a saucepan and heat slowly until steaming. Have the yolks at hand in a stainless steel bowl. Using a ladle, slowly pour some of the hot milk into the bowl with the yolks and whisk together. Now the yolks can be added to the milk in the saucepan. Pour them slowly into the milk, whisking all the while. Cook over a low flame until the custard coats the back of a spoon, or just below the point of boiling. Be careful not to spoil the custard by boiling it. Remove from the heat, add the chocolate, and stir until the chocolate is melted. Pour the chocolate custard through a wire strainer and stir in the vanilla. Cover and refrigerate until chilled.

Whip the heavy cream to soft peaks and fold into the chocolate custard. Pour the custard into the canister of an ice-cream freezer and freeze according to the manufacturer's instructions. When it is thickened and clings to the paddle in a block, spoon the ice cream into a container to freeze in your household freezer, or remove the cranking device, cork the top of the canister, repack the bucket with ice and salt, and serve directly from the canister.

Strawberry Ice Cream
Yield 3 quarts

Strawberry ice cream is too good to be enjoyed only during the unmercifully brief native berry season. Freeze your own berries by washing, draining well, hulling, and placing them on sheet pans to freeze. Fill freezer bags with the individually frozen berries, taking only what you need for a particular recipe. Thaw the berries, puree in a blender, and proceed with this recipe as if using fresh. Frozen berries are superior to those large white fruits marketed as strawberries during the winter months.

> 3 cups milk
> 2 cups sugar
> 10 egg yolks
> 1 qt fresh strawberries
> 2 cups heavy cream

✦ Put the milk and sugar into a saucepan and heat slowly until steaming. Have the yolks at hand in a stainless steel bowl. Using a ladle, slowly pour some of the hot milk into the bowl with the yolks and whisk together. Now the yolks can be added to the milk in the saucepan. Pour them slowly into the milk, whisking all the while. Cook over a low flame until the custard coats the back of a spoon, or just below the point of boiling. Be careful not to spoil the custard by boiling it. Remove from the heat and pour through a wire strainer into a bowl. Cover and refrigerate until chilled.

Wash the berries, drain until quite dry, and hull. Puree the strawberries in a blender or food processor and stir into the chilled custard. Whip the heavy cream to soft peaks. Fold into the strawberry custard. Pour into the canister of an ice-cream freezer and freeze according to the manufacturer's instructions.

When it has thickened and clings to the paddle in a block, the ice cream is done. Spoon into a container to freeze in your household freezer, or remove the cranking device, cork the top of the canister, and repack the bucket with ice and salt, and serve directly from the canister.

Strawberry Ice Cream with Brown Sugar and Sour Cream
Yield 3 quarts

Some people prefer to dress their berries with sour cream and brown sugar rather than whipped cream. This ice cream is for the epicurean whose taste favors this combination.

3 cups milk
1 cup brown sugar
1 cup white sugar
10 egg yolks
1 qt fresh strawberries
1 cup sour cream
1 cup heavy cream

✦ Follow the directions for Strawberry Ice Cream, substituting the ingredients as indicated. Stir the sour cream into chilled strawberry custard and then fold in the whipped cream. Freeze in the usual manner.

Peach Praline Ice Cream
Yield 3 quarts

Pecan brittle is pounded to a powder and swirled into peach ice cream. The resulting combination is a sweet delight.

1 cup pecans
3 cups sugar
Juice 1 lemon
3 lb fresh ripe peaches
3 cups milk
10 egg yolks
2 cups heavy cream

✦ Place 1 cup sugar and 1 teaspoon lemon juice in a saucepan. Cook over low heat until the sugar turns a light brown. Stir the pecans into the sugar and pour the mixture onto a buttered plate. When cool and hardened, place the nut brittle between two sheets of wax paper. Pound to a powder with a mallet and reserve.

Bring a large pot of water to a boil. Plunge the peaches into it, a few at a time, so that the water continues to boil. Leave in the boiling water 15–20 seconds and remove with a slotted spoon. Peel the fruit and remove the stones. Puree the peaches in a blender or food processor with the remaining lemon juice and reserve.

Put the milk and remaining 2 cups of sugar into a saucepan. Have the yolks at hand in a stainless steel bowl. Using a ladle, slowly pour some of the hot milk into the bowl with the yolks and whisk together. Now the yolks can be added to the milk in the saucepan. Pour them slowly into the milk, whisking all the while. Cook over low heat until the custard coats the back of a spoon, or just below the point of boiling. Do not spoil the custard by boiling it.

Remove from the heat and pour through a wire strainer into a bowl. Cover and refrigerate until chilled. Stir the pureed peaches into the chilled custard. Whip the heavy cream to soft peaks and fold into the peach custard. Pour into the canister of an ice-cream freezer and freeze according to the manufacturer's instructions.

When it has thickened and clings to the paddle in a block, the ice cream is done. Pour in the praline powder and run the machine just long enough to disperse the candy throughout the ice cream. Spoon the ice cream into a container to freeze in your household freezer, or remove the cranking device, cork the top of the canister, repack the bucket with ice and salt, and serve directly from the canister.

Pumpkin Ice Cream
Yield 3 quarts

This richly colored orange ice cream, flecked with spices and flavored with maple syrup, will remind you of pumpkin pie.

3 cups milk
10 egg yolks
2 cups maple syrup
1 tsp cinnamon
1 tsp ground ginger
1 tsp nutmeg
2 cups pumpkin puree, or one 16-oz can of prepared pumpkin
2 cups heavy cream

✦ Put the milk and spices into a saucepan and heat slowly until steaming. Have the yolks at hand in a stainless steel bowl. Using a ladle, slowly pour some of the hot milk into the bowl with the yolks and whisk together. Now the yolks can be added to the milk in the saucepan. Pour them slowly into the milk, whisking all the while. Cook over a low flame until the custard will coat the back of a spoon, or just below the point of boiling. Be careful not to spoil the custard by boiling it.

Remove from the heat and pour through a wire strainer into a bowl. Add the maple syrup and pumpkin puree, cover, and refrigerate until chilled.

Whip the heavy cream to soft peaks and fold into the pumpkin custard. Pour into the canister of an ice-cream freezer and freeze according to the manufacturer's instructions.

When it has thickened and clings to the paddle in a block, the ice cream is done. Spoon it into a container to freeze in your household freezer, or remove the cranking device, cork the top of the canister, repack the bucket with ice and salt, and serve directly from the canister.

Liqueurs

✦

Wild Strawberry Liqueur

Rose Petal Liqueur

Raspberry Liqueur

Spiced Chocolate Liqueur

Lemon Liqueur

Maple Liqueur

How to Make Your Own Liqueurs

Liqueurs require little preparation time but lots of patience. Once you have combined the alcohol, sugar syrup, and flavoring agent, you must wait up to a month before sampling the result.

Almost any fruit, spice, herb, or flower can be used, alone or in concert, to produce original and commercially unavailable potions. Homemade liqueurs make thoughtful gifts yet are inexpensive and simple to prepare.

Place the sealed vessel containing your preparation in a dark place. Shake it every few days to encourage the dispersal and absorption of flavors. Strain the mixture after the storage period has elapsed. This operation transforms the jar full of berries or flower petals into a beautifully transparent liquid. This is not difficult but requires the patience of Job. You must leave the mixture alone. If you try to force it, you will end up with sediment and suspended particles in the finished product.

Strain the liquid in stages. Pour some of the mixture into a wire strainer lined with a paper coffee filter before you go to bed at night or leave for work in the morning. Repeat the process as necessary. Then transfer the finished liqueur to a decanter or a special gift bottle.

Wild Strawberry Liqueur
Yield 1 quart 8 oz (5 cups)

Domesticated strawberries were bred from the plant that produces these pea-sized wild fruits. Though science creates larger and larger berries, something is lost along the way. The fragrance and spicy flavor of the tiny wild berries put them in a class by themselves.

Wild strawberries thrive in open fields and pastures. Their diminutive size precludes using them in most recipes. The time and labor for picking is simply too much. Wild strawberry liqueur is the perfect way to get the most from your efforts.

1 pint wild strawberries, or 1 qt native strawberries
1 cup sugar
½ cup water
Zest and juice 1 lemon
1 fifth 100-proof vodka

✦ Put the sugar and water in a saucepan. Bring to a boil and simmer until the syrup is clear, about 1 minute. Remove from the heat and cool to room temperature before proceeding with the recipe.

One may mix wild and native strawberries. Wash the berries and drain until quite dry. Hull and place in a large glass jar with the other ingredients and seal tightly. Leave in a dark place—a closet will do—for 1 month. Shake the jar periodically.

Strain the liqueur through cheesecloth and squeeze to extract the liquid. Line a wire strainer with a paper coffee filter. Pour the liqueur into the strainer and leave it alone for a long as it takes to drip through. Replace the filter when it becomes clogged. The tiny particles are thus removed, leaving only the essence of the strawberries. Store the finished liqueur in a decanter or a tightly sealed bottle.

Rose Petal Liqueur
Yield 1 quart 8 oz (5 cups)

Long after the chimneys collapsed and cellar holes filled in, evidence of earlier inhabitants survives. Gnarled and twisted apple trees, lilac bushes, and wild roses continue to thrive on the sites of old homesteads. The blooms of old-fashioned rose bushes are thick with petals and have a spicy air. Use them as a flavoring for a delicately scented liqueur. Its surprising flavor echoes the fragrance.

1 cup sugar
½ cup water
3 cups unsprayed rose petals, well packed
1 fifth 100-proof vodka
Juice and zest ½ lemon

✦ It is essential to use unsprayed roses for this liqueur, which could be deadly made from petals treated with chemicals. Old-fashioned roses have a more pronounced and somewhat spicier fragrance than hybrid tea roses. They are very common in gardens throughout New England as well as on old building sites.

Put the sugar and water in a saucepan. Bring to a boil and simmer until the syrup is clear, about 1 minute. Remove from the heat and cool to room temperature before proceeding with the recipe.

Collect the petals from wild or unsprayed domestic roses. The liqueur becomes the color of the roses you use. Pink ones seem to give the nicest and most characteristic result. Place the petals in a jar with the other ingredients, seal tightly, and leave in a dark place for 4 days. Shake the jar every day. The petals become colorless and translucent as their essence is absorbed by the liquor.

Strain the liqueur through cheesecloth, squeezing to extract the liquid. Line a wire strainer with a paper coffee filter. Pour the liqueur into the strainer and leave it alone for as long as it takes to drip through. Replace the filter when it becomes clogged. Rose petal liqueur has very little in the way of suspended particles so this operation requires much less time than some other liqueurs. Store the finished liqueur in a decanter or a tightly sealed bottle.

Raspberry Liqueur
Yield about 1 quart 8 oz (5 cups)

Try this liqueur with red, golden, purple, or black raspberries. Each variety has a distinct taste and fragrance. A basket containing small bottles of liqueur made from each color berry makes a unique gift.

1 qt fresh raspberries
1 cup sugar
½ cup water
1 fifth 100-proof vodka

✦ Put the sugar and water in a saucepan. Bring to a boil and simmer until the syrup is clear, about 1 minute. Remove from the heat and cool to room temperature before proceeding with the recipe.

Raspberries need not be washed, unless they have been sprayed, since they grow so high above the ground. If you purchase raspberries, washing is a good practice as most commercial produce has been treated with chemicals. Place the berries in a large glass jar with the other ingredients, seal tightly, and leave in a dark place such as a closet for 1 month. Shake the jar periodically.

Strain the liqueur through cheesecloth, squeezing to extract the liquid.

Line a wire strainer with a paper coffee filter. Pour the liqueur into the strainer and leave it alone for as long as it takes to drip through. Replace the filter when it becomes clogged. The tiny particles are removed leaving only the essence of the raspberries. Store the finished liqueur in a decanter or a tightly sealed bottle.

Spiced Chocolate Liqueur
Yield 1 quart 5 oz (5 cups)

Chocolate, cinnamon, and orange peel make this liqueur a dessert all by itself. Add a teaspoon or two of cream to a serving for a cream liqueur.

> **2 cups sugar**
> **1 cup water**
> **1 fifth 100-proof vodka**
> **¼ cup cocoa powder**
> **1 vanilla bean, split lengthwise**
> **1 Tbsp instant coffee**
> **1 stick cinnamon**
> **Zest and juice 1 orange**
> **Pinch mace**

✦ Put the sugar, water, cinnamon, mace, and orange zest in a saucepan. Bring to a boil and simmer slowly for 5 minutes, then remove from the heat. Add the coffee and vanilla bean. Put the cocoa powder in a heat-proof bowl. Pour the hot syrup into it a little at a time, stirring all the while so the powder does not form lumps. Cool to room temperature. Pour into a jar, add the orange juice and vodka, seal tightly, and leave the jar in a dark place for 2 weeks. Shake the jar periodically.

Strain the liqueur through a cheesecloth, squeezing to extract the liquid. Line a wire strainer with a paper coffee filter. Pour the liqueur into the strainer and leave it alone for as long as it takes to drip through. Residue from the cocoa powder must be removed. You will need to change the filter a half dozen or more times to accomplish this. The liqueur may take several days to strain if you are leaving it to drip while you sleep or work. Store the finished liqueur in a decanter or a tightly sealed bottle.

Lemon Liqueur
Yield about 1 quart 8 oz (5 cups)

In summer store this liqueur in your freezer. When you serve it, the tiny glasses will frost over from contact with the icy liquid.

1¼ cups sugar
1 cup lemon juice (4–5 lemons)
Zest 1 lemon
1 fifth 100-proof vodka

✦ Put the sugar, lemon juice, and zest in a saucepan. Bring to a boil and simmer until clear, about 1 minute. Remove from the heat and cool to room temperature before proceeding with the recipe. Pour the syrup and vodka into a large glass jar. Place the jar in a dark place for 1 week, shaking the jar periodically.

Strain the liqueur through a cheesecloth, squeezing to extract the liquid. Line a wire strainer with a paper coffee filter. Pour the liqueur into the strainer and leave it alone for as long as it takes to drip through. There is very little sediment in this liqueur so the process will proceed quickly. Store the finished liqueur in a decanter or a tightly sealed bottle.

Maple Liqueur
Yield about 1 quart

I have never found maple liqueur in a store, though I don't know why. There is a concoction based on Scotch and another distilled from maple syrup. Oddly, neither tastes like maple. This recipe is the easiest imaginable, tastes exactly as you would expect, and can be made minutes before serving.

1 cup maple syrup
1 fifth 100-proof vodka

✦ Combine the vodka and maple syrup. Pour into a decanter or a tightly sealed bottle. The liqueur is ready to serve at once.

Further Reading

✦

Duffy, John. *Vermont: An Illustrated History*. Northridge, Vt.: produced in cooperation with the Vermont Historical Society and Windsor Publications, 1985. Large format. Duffy's concise, narrative style comes alive with scores of illustrations and photographs. Like old gazetteers, a history of the book's sponsors are included.

Gibbons, Euell. *Stalking the Wild Asparagus*. Putney, Vt.: Alan C. Hood, 1987. A classic book on the recognition, gathering, preparation, and use of the natural foods that grow wild all about us. Contains many detailed and tasty recipes.

Kent, Louise Andrews. *Mrs. Appleyard's Kitchen*. Montpelier, Vt.: Vermont Life Magazine, 1977. "Some of the best reading in the world," Mrs. Appleyard says, "is found in cookbooks." Her book proves the point. Conversational style runs the gamut of food preparation.

Lewis, Anne. *Vermont Foods: History and Preparation*. Proctor, Vt.: Wilson Castle, 1982. A slim edition analyzing the reasons Vermont cuisine developed, supported by overview of traditional preparations.

Miller, Orson K. *Mushrooms of North America*. New York: E. P. Dutton,

1979. Small enough for use as a field guide. Simple, easy-to-read format, 422 species described, 292 color photographs. If you must buy only one mushroom book, this is the one.

Peterson, Lee Allen. *A Field Guide to Edible Wild Plants (Eastern/Central North America)*. Boston: Houghton Mifflin, 1977. Finding an unknown plant is quickly accomplished. Edible parts are described, method of preparation explained.

Pixley, Aristene. *Vermont Country Cooking*. [Reprint *The Green Mountain Cookbook* 1941.] New York: Dover, 1979. Recipes assume that the cook knows his/her way around the kitchen. Solid compilation of Vermont classics.

Index

✦